The Literacy Leadership Team
Sustaining and Expanding Success

Kathy S. Froelich

Florida State University

Enrique A. Puig

University of Central Florida

Allyn & Bacon

Boston   New York   San Francisco
Mexico City   Montreal   Toronto   London   Madrid   Munich   Paris
Hong Kong   Singapore   Tokyo   Cape Town   Sydney

I dedicate this book to my husband Flip for his continued support,
to Dr. Marilyn J. Young for being my lifelong friend and mentor,
and to my colleagues Dr. Susan Wood and Dr. Pamela "Sissi" Carroll—
Susan for being a calm voice in the storm and Sissi for lighting my way. —KSF

As always, as in all my endeavors, I dedicate this work of passion
to Robert C. Mumby Jr., Alexandre E. Puig, Raquel Puig, and all my friends and family
who have supported me through hours of reading and writing. —EAP

Executive Editor: Aurora Martínez Ramos
Series Editorial Assistant: Kara Kikel
Executive Marketing Manager: Krista Clark
Marketing Manager: Danae April
Production Editor: Paula Carroll
Editorial Production Service: Lynda Griffiths
Composition Buyer: Linda Cox
Manufacturing Buyer: Megan Cochran
Electronic Composition: SchneckDePippo Graphics
Interior Design: SchneckDePippo Graphics
Cover Administrator: Linda Knowles

For Professional Development resources visit www.allynbaconmerrill.com.

Between the time website information is gathered and then published, it is not unusual for some sites to have closed. Also, the transcription of URLs can result in typographical errors. The publisher would appreciate notification where these errors occur so that they may be corrected in subsequent editions.

Printed in the United States of America

10 9 8 7 6 5 4 3 2 1   12 11 10 09 08

**Allyn & Bacon
is an imprint of**

PEARSON

ISBN-10:   0-205-56992-7
ISBN-13: 978-0-205-56992-2

Contents

Section Three Utilizing Scaffolds to Expand Success 123

Preface

In 2003, at the 48th Annual International Reading Association Conference in Orlando, Florida, Catherine Snow from Harvard University delivered a presentation to a room full of internationally recognized scholars on the concept of *distributed cognition*. We came away with the concept that distributed cognition, in the context of Snow's presentation, is the idea that we can't all know everything about everything. We are all dependent on the knowledge and experiences of others to accomplish certain tasks in our busy lives. Doctors take care of our bodies. Accountants and bankers assist us with our finances. Lawyers defend and protect our civil rights. The list of how we distribute cognition is endless, since we cannot possibly know everything we need to know for our daily lives to function fluidly. Our thinking and expertise have to be focused and collaborative. This insight applies directly to the daily function of schools, too. Although we recognize that the school principal is a cornerstone for literacy leadership in a school, we respectfully and admirably understand that it is virtually impossible for she or he to know everything that there is to know about learning and instruction.

Keeping Snow's idea of distributed cognition at the forefront, we propose that this concept is the driving force behind literacy leadership teams. Generally, literacy leadership teams are created with a healthy respect for diversity and experiences. Most literacy leadership teams are made up of classroom teachers, support personnel, administration, students (in some cases), and a proficient literacy coach. With the support of literacy coaches as lead learners, literacy leadership teams can certainly take schools from successful to significant. We strongly hold the belief that literacy coaches are the lead learners that should guide literacy leadership teams, and because of this, we designed this book as a companion volume to *The Literacy Coach: Guiding in the Right Direction* (Puig & Froelich, 2007).

The idea of leadership teams is certainly not a new concept in education or business. Historically, the question always comes up regarding input and professional learning of the leadership team. In this book, we propose that the literacy leadership team take its lead for professional learning from the school's literacy coach. Of course, in order for the literacy coach to be considered a lead learner and guide for the team, she or he must have a clear picture of the school's strengths and challenges as well as personal credibility, respect, and admiration of colleagues. For this to take place, we go back to our belief that a proficient literacy coach is akin to an ethnographer collecting artifacts, either as a participant or nonparticipant of the observations (Puig & Froelich, 2007), so that she or he is able to assist the literacy leadership team in making informed decisions to sustain and expand success.

We believe that many school literacy initiatives fall short over time because there was never a long-term, ongoing, job-embedded plan in place. In *The Literacy Leadership Team: Sustaining and Expanding Success*, we provide specific information to assist not only the literacy coach as a lead learner but we also help the entire literacy leadership team to focus on positive change, or forward shifts. Our experience has taught us that a pivotal starting point for a literacy leadership team is to develop a common language and understanding about literacy processing and adult learners.

Without this foundational knowledge, it seems unlikely that a literacy leadership team will recognize critical data that will influence learning and instruction in a positive manner. The team has to have this understanding to be able to formulate a theory of what is occurring and how to interact with what is occurring by utilizing the teams distributed and collective cognition. Each team member will bring a wealth of personalized knowledge and experiences that the team will need to acknowledge and use as a seed for thinking in different directions so that team members are better able to support the school as a place of learning for everyone. Everyone comes to the metaphoric table with what Gonzalez, Moll, and Amanti (2005) call "funds of knowledge."

To support teams in building the necessary foundational knowledge, this book addresses literacy as a process in elementary classrooms and across content area classrooms in middle and high school. Furthermore, going beyond this foundational knowledge, it is also critical that all team members understand what conditions of learning need to be present to motivate and engage learners of all ages.

Many articles and books have been written on literacy leadership and leadership teams. Very little has been written on the development and function of *literacy leadership teams,* particularly on literacy leadership teams that adopt and utilize an ethnographic perspective as a primary function led by a literacy coach. Most of what has been written on literacy leadership teams is limited to brief subsections, chapters, and articles. Certainly, the literature on literacy leadership and leadership teams impacts the development of literacy leadership teams, but the fact remains that an organizational framework and the daily operation of the team in a school setting have seldom been addressed in a book solely dedicated to the topic. *The Literacy Leadership Team: Sustaining and Expanding Success* is grounded in theory with practical recommendations to create an organizational framework and support the daily work of a literacy leadership team where it matters most—the school setting.

We respectfully acknowledge the meta-analysis of the National Reading Panel (2000) and purposefully have chosen to not include it in this text for a couple of reasons. One is that we included information from it in *The Literacy Coach: Guiding in the Right Direction* (2007). Our second reason is that the NRP report is a well-distributed document that has been read by many educators since its publication in 2000.

If educators want schools to be places of learning and instruction for all (Craig, 2006; Tharp & Gallimore, 1988), we have to put in place a system with built-in safety nets where errors are viewed as half-rights. Lyons and Pinnell (2001) tell us that forward shifts rarely occur because of one person or even a few people, including the principal and the literacy coach. To create true forward shifts in schools, the creation of a literacy leadership team is essential for implementing an on-site system at the whole school level to sustain and expand success (Knight & Stallings, 1995; Maden & Hillman, 1996; Darling-Hammond, 1997; Hill & Crevola, 1998; Langer, 2000; Maden, 2001). Furthermore, for this system to be in place, a dynamic literacy leadership team with distributed experiences and knowledge guided by a highly qualified literacy coach as a lead learner is paramount (Craig, 2006; Ross, 1992; Veenman & Denessen, 2001; Booth & Rowsell, 2002). *The Literacy Leadership Team: Sustaining and Expanding Success* provides clear and practical time-proven practices to assure that schools are consistently developing an "informed eye."

Acknowledgments

We would like to acknowledge the following "cast of thousands" for expanding our knowledge of literacy leadership teams over a period of many years that assisted us in writing this text: our editor, Aurora Martínez, for guidance and her belief in the project; the Literacy Collaborative staff at the Ohio State University, especially Andrea McCarrier and Carol Lyons; Gay Su Pinnell for being a muse, friend, and colleague; Irene Fountas and the Literacy Collaborative staff at Lesley University; Susan Taylor and Connie Parrish with the Literacy Collaborative at Georgia State University; Diane E. Deford at the University of South Carolina, who to date remains the quintessential model for a literacy coach; Denise N. Morgan at Kent State University for keeping touch and being a supportive, encouraging friend; Sarah Mahurt at Purdue University and the wealth of literacy coordinators and teams in Goshen, Indiana; Katie Button and Jan Bogard at Texas Tech University; the dedicated crème de la crème of literacy coaches in Orange County Public Schools and Seminole County Public Schools, Florida; Carol Hagemann, Cathy Rivera, Kori Moore, Susan Kelly, Jacqui Oester, Yvonne Williams, Pat Schiavoni, Gina Fugnitto, Betsy McClure, Kay Dusich, Hattie Summers, Debra Goodwin, Jan Lacey, Gail Kirkland, Shirley Martin, and Dixie Turner, all of whom have provided extensive in-service to literacy leadership teams and were more than willing to share their experiences; Lee Foster, Maxie Cinammon, and Ruthenia Ward for vision and faith in Reading Recovery® as a viable and cost-effective immediate intensive intervention to support low-progress readers; Vicky J. Brooks for believing in the Literacy Collaborative's ongoing, job-embedded professional development and how it helps teachers and students realize the power of becoming literate through good initial instruction; Julie Teal and Sandy Ward for being "critical friends," Reading Recovery® teacher leaders, and colleagues constantly supporting and encouraging.

We are also eternally grateful to the state of Florida and the Just Read, Florida! office for its ongoing support of reading/literacy leadership teams throughout the state that has provided us with incredible insights into how to sustain and expand success in schools. A special thanks to Barbara (Bo) Elzie, Cari Miller, Melinda Webster, Laurie Lee, and Kevin Smith. We owe a very warm and special thank you to Evan B. Lefsky for his perspective and contribution of Chapter 12 that enriched this text.

Our acknowledgments would certainly not be complete without recognizing Dean Sandra L. Robinson at the University of Central Florida and all the Florida Literacy and Reading Excellence (FLaRE) Center area coordinators at the University of Central Florida: Susan Kelly, Marcia Halpin, Roxana Hurtado, April Johnson, Connie Cain, Larry Bedebaugh, Linda Tuschinksi (and Dickie), Cathi Addison, Christine Futrell-Harris, Amy Abate, Kathy Baich, Charla Bauer, Kris Bray, Marlene Cabrera, Joe Cloutier, Carmen Concepcion, Craig Cosden, Cheree Davis, Jocelyn Downs, Jennifer Escandell, Cheryle Ferlita, Donna Garcia, Darliny Gonzalez-Katz, Nancy Lewis, Karen McDaniels, Julie Anne McEachin, Pam Rader, Ruth Shaulis, Renee Walton; and our colleagues with Reading

First Professional Development at the University of Central Florida: Luanne P. Nelson, Carol Norton, Karen Ladinsky, Dawn Bingham, Hatti Brown, Leyda Caride, Pam Chalfant, Cathy Constantine, Katy Cortelyou, Carol Cron, Connie Dierking, Nikki Jones Yvette Lerner, Vivian McClain, Ann Melder, Vicki Paige, Evelyn Prakash, Tammy Ruhl, Eyvonne Ryan, Verna Smith, Jan Stiers, Ruthie Teets, Pam Vickaryous, and Hope Walker. We thank Pamela S. Craig for sharing her dissertation and research with us to support many of our claims. In addition we want to thank the FLaRE Faculty Fellows (Thyria Ansley/FAMU, Deb Harris/FAU, Linda Ray/FGCU, Pat Wachholz/FGCU, Joyce Fine/FIU, Kent Butler/UCF, Vicky Zygouris-Coe/UCF, Zhihui Fang/UF, Wanda Hedrick/UNF, Lunetta Williams/UNF, Nancy Williams/USF, Gwen Senokossoff/USF-St. Pete, Charlotte Boling/UWF, and Kathleen Heubach/UWF) for sharing their knowledge and experiences that contributed to this text. A special thank you is also due to David Booth for introducing us to the work of Kieran Egan. We especially acknowledge all the classroom teachers and administrators who have invited us into their literacy leadership teams and shared with us their adaptive challenges and successes.

We extend our gratitude to the following reviewers: Jennifer L. Blecha, Widewater Elementary School; Joy L. Brown, Stafford County Public Schools; Nancy DeVries Guth, Stafford County Public Schools; Vicki Jirash, Howe Public School; Barbara Mintzer, Peter Muschal Elementary School; and Kirsten Steis, Stafford County Public Schools.

Ultimately, we thank with the utmost respect and admiration the work of Brian Cambourne and the late Marie M. Clay for their extraordinary research and endeavors. Through their powerful words and passion, they have changed the face of learning and instruction.

Foreword

If I were given a mandate to establish and organize a literacy program for a school, I would begin by reading and internalizing this comprehensive and thoughtful book, *The Literacy Leadership Team: Sustaining and Expanding Success*. The two experienced and wise authors, Kathy Froelich and Enrique Puig, have set out a detailed framework for developing, implementing, and sustaining a literacy leadership team that would move a school literacy program forward into success for all students. It is one goal to demand that the staff and administration of a school have a mandate for excellence in literacy achievement, but it is an entirely different matter for a school to develop a philosophy of and a pedagogy for creating an overarching framework for affecting real change in literacy education and instruction. This book offers educators a schema for success in establishing a schoolwide structure for effectively supporting all students in their growth toward becoming literate citizens, by creating a carefully constructed, well-informed, collegial literacy leadership team.

The authors stress the power of a representative and respected working team, a collaborative and cooperative committee of classroom teachers, support personnel, administrators, students, along with an informed and effective literacy coach who can guide the group toward positive change and significant movement. Froelich and Puig explore the conditions that schools need to establish in order to support and engage the staff in promoting literacy behaviors and practices for their students that will lead to literacy proficiency for everyone.

This book presents an action plan for literacy change, based on the authors' experiences, practice, and research, and supported by the work of recognized authorities in the field. It offers information and motivation for clarifying the mission of a school literacy leadership team, and presents educators with procedures and plans for implementing its mandate for building capacity, for sustaining professional learning, for understanding literacy processing and instructional practice, for utilizing resources and expanding success, and for building an ongoing, job-embedded, professional learning community.

I appreciate so many enriching aspects of this book, from the scenarios that begin each chapter, vignettes of school life that cause us to confront our own assumptions and biases, to the thoughtful and mindful reflections at the end of each chapter that help us focus on our own school situations and possibilities. As well, the annotated bibliography represents supportive readings to extend our understanding of the many complex facets of effective literacy change.

Through their study, their research, and their writing, the authors have assisted us in developing our own literacy leadership teams so that we can meet the needs of our own particular school situations. They have taught us that everything and everyone matter in the quest for literacy. Administrators, teachers, support staff, students, and, I would add, parents, must all be actively engaged in the literacy mandate, guided by the literacy coach and supported by the leadership literacy team. I am grateful for this book: It offers us an enlightening and workable framework for building a schoolwide program for accomplishing the dream of literacy success for our all of our students.

David Booth
Professor Emeritus, Scholar in Residence
The Ontario Institute for Studies in Education
University of Toronto

Introduction

Our earlier book, *The Literacy Coach: Guiding in the Right Direction* (2007) examined what it takes to be a successful coach in today's schools. It laid the foundation for understanding professional learning, literacy coaching, and its impact on literacy leadership teams from a different perspective by looking at the history of professional learning. In that text, we explored what models work best for teachers to promote forward shifts in learning and instruction. We looked at what it takes to learn and how to use observational lens. Taking an ethnographic perspective on literacy coaching, we addressed taking field notes and understanding the protocols that help literacy coaches, teachers, and principals become co-learners.

Three types of categories for literacy coaching—coaching for aesthetics, coaching for procedures, and coaching for rationales—were developed in addition to exploring how literacy coaches move from presenters of information to co-researchers/learners. Because we believe that the success of any professional learning program relies on principals as well as teachers, we looked at their role and what kinds of support make for strong school reforms. We strongly suggest reading *The Literacy Coach: Guiding in the Right Direction* to support and expand your interpretations of *The Literacy Leadership Team: Sustaining and Expanding Success*.

In this book, we present a triadic model for literacy leadership teams to sustain and expand success that relies on (1) creating a foundation to sustain success, (2) assembling a working system to promote forward shifts or positive change, and (3) utilizing scaffolds to expand success. The model addresses the development of the literacy leadership team as part of a support system to build capacity and to sustain professional learning with the focus on improving student learning. It serves as a blueprint to guide school literacy leadership teams in collaboratively investigating and seeking solutions to issues of student learning and professional learning. Thought-provoking cases and guides are provided throughout the text to encourage conversations and to support school teams in improving student learning. A primary focus of this book is that schools and school personnel need to take a broad-spectrum perspective that school is a place of learning for all (Tharp & Gallimore, 1988).

In the first section, we address the theoretical understandings that are necessary to sustain literacy leadership teams over time. Because we want to build strong literacy leadership teams, we must first understand how adults learn. Using Malcolm Knowles's (1978) seminal work on andragogy, Chapter 1 examines adult learning principles and how andragogy differs from pedagogy, a traditional model used with most learners.

We believe that there are fundamental characteristics that learners need in order to be successful. Chapter 2 focuses on these characteristics. Using Brian Cambourne's conditions of learning, the chapter incorporates these features and applies them to adult learners.

Over time, we have learned that developing a common language is a critical element in the development of effective literacy leadership teams. In Chapter 3, terms are introduced as a springboard for discussion to support each other in investigating a variety of themes to improve instruction.

Chapter 4 explores literacy processing. Reading and writing are viewed as corequisite processes with fundamental features that learners must use to be successful. The chapter also looks at ways to sustain literate enterprises and expand meaning through the reciprocity of literate activities.

Chapter 5 sets the ground work for building strong literacy leadership teams. Using the work of theorists such as Peter Senge, Ann Liebermann, Ellen R. Stahl, Matthew B. Miles, and others, we identify the criteria for a supportive and effective team member, and how we put these people together so that they can support effective, ongoing, and consistent forward shifts. Finally, the chapter shows two models of leadership teams: an elementary (pre-K to grade 5) model and a secondary (grades 6–12) model.

The second section in our triadic model of implementation addresses the assembling of a working system by the literacy leadership team to promote forward shifts. In this section, specific action steps are presented. We acknowledge that formal and informal assessment is always the engine that drives the solution-seeking train. This is true when we try to actualize needs and challenges within the school setting. Chapter 6 uses appropriate assessment to guide our investigations and appropriate evaluation to help guide our practice. After identifying an initial adaptive challenge, we address investigating the theme or concern. Chapter 7 relies on reading and understanding the literature about literacy leadership teams and how these teams might further the goal of sustainable literacy practices through change. In Chapter 8, we address refining an adaptive challenge or concern so that the team can focus on literacy processing and instructional practices to support learning.

One way in which a team can operate within the school setting is through the development of a study group to support reflection and future directions. Chapter 9 discusses the elements needed to build a study group, how the group can reach consensus on issues, and such things as how to choose appropriate texts for study.

The third section of the book involves utilizing resources as scaffolds to expand success. Chapters 10 and 11 present ways to develop ongoing, job-embedded professional learning as well as a schoolwide plan. Chapter 10 also looks at a five-stage professional learning plan focused on improving instruction.

Although many literacy leadership teams exist without state or district support, we have found that when teams seek and draw support from the state and district it increases the likelihood for sustaining and expanding success. For this reason, we asked Evan B. Lefsky, the executive director of the Just Read, Florida! office to contribute Chapter 12 to assist us in understanding how statewide initiatives can support schools in developing literacy leadership teams.

At the beginning of each chapter we provide examples of school experiences we call "'X-ed' Change" scenarios to be read and explored before actually reading the chapter. These are real-life situations that we have experienced firsthand in schools and among groups that "X" out (or prevent) change from occurring. Although the "'X-ed' Change" scenarios may come across as negative, we see them as real learning opportunities that have shaped our thinking in a positive manner. One can learn from challenges if one addresses them honestly and view them for future adaptations. After reading each chapter you are asked to discuss questions about how you and your team members can "exchange" the elements that limited or prohibited change so that positive change or forward shifts can take place. We add a brief case study, or libretto, with reflection questions to consider at the end of each chapter as well. An annotated bibliography of supportive literature is provided at the end of the book to help the literacy leadership team define issues and agendas to be addressed in team meetings.

We hope you will find *The Literacy Leadership Team: Sustaining and Expanding Success* an effective tool to help build your school's strong, successful literacy leadership team, one that has improving and sustaining appropriate learning practices for all students and teachers as its primary mission.

We have written this book as a "braided conversation" for administrators, literacy coaches, and teacher colleagues. At times it may appear that we are addressing a particular stakeholder or the literacy leadership team, but that is not the case. In each and every chapter, we are speaking to administrators, literacy coaches, and teacher colleagues—essential members of the literacy leadership team. Extrapolating from Rosenblatt (1994), each reader will create his or her own "poem" from reading this book and will enrich his or her interpretation by engaging in many conversations over time with like-minded colleagues interested in creating a literacy leadership team to improve learning and instruction.

Creating a Foundation to Sustain Success

We have found that without a strong theoretical foundation, most literacy initiatives in a school setting waiver and wane over time. In order for literacy leadership teams to sustain success, they need to have a strong theoretical understanding—in other words, understanding the compelling "whys." In this section, we will investigate some theoretical constructs that will provide literacy leadership teams the necessary language to promote accurate analysis of assessments and to support appropriate instructional practices to tackle specific adaptive challenges. Some of the challenges that literacy leadership teams encounter when implementing change are dealing with adult colleagues in a professional, respectful, and sensitive manner; supporting and replicating literate environments; communicating with a common language; and understanding how students process information to improve learning and instruction. With a strong theoretical foundation, most of those challenges can be brought to the table and adapted to fulfill a school's need in improving learning and instruction.

Although we have relied on the work of Malcolm Knowles, Brian Cambourne, and Marie Clay (just to mention a few) as a foundation to support the structure of a literacy leadership team, no body of scholarly work can provide all the answers to all adaptive challenges that a school may need to tackle. It is up to the literacy leadership team, with the support of a knowledgeable literacy coach, to evaluate its school's needs, and to use the information in this section and transform it from theory to practice. Although you may be tempted to skip this section, please do not. It is vital!

Chapter 1

Understanding Adult Learners

"X-ed" Change

Ms. Jarrod: Please get in your seats everyone so that we can begin the meeting on time. If we don't start on time, I will have to keep everyone until we are finished and you know some people will not be happy about that. And could we all settle down and not make so much noise? Did someone see Mr. Peres outside? Could you ask him to come in and find his group? I can't believe that I have to start each meeting this way, people. Come on now. We have a lot of work to do to get prepared for the upcoming open house and we have to talk about the new state testing requirements. Could someone close the door? If anyone is still outside they will just have to stay there until we take our 10-minute break. I can't wait any longer to start.

Ms. Parks: I don't know why she treats us this way. Every time we have these meetings I feel like I am one of my own students, not an educator with 20 years of teaching experience. I thought when we got rid of Mr. Crandall we would be treated with a little more respect, but Mrs. Jarrod treats us like 6-year-olds.

Mr. Dans: I think she's actually worse. She can't get over that "herding" mentality and she is so condescending. I thought she taught high school, not elementary school. What do you think this "group" thing is all about?

Ms. Parks: I heard that we are going to be divided into some kind of "study teams" that will have teachers from each department. What we are going to be expected to do, I don't have a clue. It should be interesting.

Ms. Jarrod: Okay, everyone, I have given a list of the groups to all department heads and they will tell you which group you will be in and what items you will be reviewing for today's meeting. We will break up into groups now and come back together in one hour for each group's report. "Okay, are there any questions? Mr. Baines?

Mr. Baines: Ms. Jarrod, what exactly are we going to be looking at in these groups?

Ms. Jarrod: Don't worry—your group leader will let you know. Now please, get into those groups!

Mr. Baines: You asked if we had questions. Why can't you at least give us an overview of what this new program is all about?

Ms. Jarrod: I don't want to take the time to go over what your group leader will go over with you. Now get into groups.

In this situation, the principal, Ms. Jarrod, has established several points that are contradictive to adult learning theory. After reading this chapter you will see the "Exchange" section at the end with several reflection questions to consider.

As schools move away from a "top-down" model of learning and move into one of "community of learners" (Sergiovanni, 2000; Lent, 2007), the literacy leadership team will play a vital role in bridging the divide between the administration and faculty, the faculty and parents, and the faculty and students. Along with a knowledgeable literacy coach, these literacy leadership teams will be the conduit that will allow for sustainable positive change or forward shifts in learning and instruction. Because adult learners differ from their younger counterparts in a number of ways, we need to examine just what these differences are. Literacy leadership teams need to understand the different dynamics that make up the adult learner so that there is a seamless transition from individual to group learning.

Andragogy

In essence, *andragogy* is the art and science of learning and instruction with adults. We are all different and we have different reasons for learning. As adults, we don't need the same learning experiences from our "teachers" as younger learners. We don't need the constant attention to facts and details that our younger counterparts might. We bring years of life experiences to bear on the learning environment and we can pick and choose when we want to engage in intentional learning.

Based on the seminal work of John Dewey, Eduard C. Lindeman (1961) was a driving force in developing a theory for adult learning. He did not differentiate between the adult learner and the "child" learner; rather, he saw it as those in adult learning environments versus those in "conventional" ones. He stated:

> Authoritative teaching, examination which precludes original thinking, rigid pedagogical formulae—all these have no place in adult education. . . . Small groups of aspiring adults who desire to keep their minds fresh and vigorous, who begin to learn by confronting pertinent situations, who dig down into the reservoirs of their experience before resorting to texts and secondary facts, who are led in the discussion by teachers who are also searchers after wisdom and not oracles: this constitutes the setting for adult education, the modern quest for life's meaning.

Linderman (1961) went on to say that he saw adult education as a "new technique for learning," one in which the learner can examine his or her life's experiences and evaluate them. He concluded by saying, "My conception of adult education is this: a cooperative venture in non-authoritarian, informal learning, the chief purpose of which is to discover the meaning of experience." Lindeman assumed five things about adult learners: (1) they are motivated to learn because they want to explore the needs and interests that only learning can satisfy, (2) learning has a life-centered orientation, (3) experience is the foundation for all learning, (4) learning as adults should be self-directed, and (5) our differences only increase as we get older.

Building on Lindeman's fundamental premise, Malcolm Knowles, the "father" of adult learning theory, refined the term *andragogy*. When he first used the term, he meant it to mean a way of assisting adult learners in making appropriate choices for furthering their education. Initially, he believed that andragogy was the opposite end of the continuum from pedagogy (Knowles, 1978). He later realized that pedagogy and andragogy were points along a similar continuum, with six underlying principles that govern the adult learner: (1) a need to "know," (2) the learner's view of herself or himself, (3) prior background knowledge of the learner, (4) how ready the learner is, (5) an orientation to learning, and (6) motivation to learn (Knowles, Holton, & Swanson, 2005).

What we as learners need to know is based on the "who, what, and why" of learning. We determine what content is important. We see ourselves as self-directed learners (Knowles, Holton, & Swanson, 2005), meaning that we can determine what is to be learned, how we learn, as well as being able to distinguish between learning that is relevant, meaningful, and rich and that which is superficial and limited. Adult learners rely on a wealth of experiences and have a broad schema for individual tasks. We can relate the learning environment to our personal environment. Our learning mirrors our lives. Learning for us is based on a need to solve problems and is reliant on the context of the material to be learned. There has to be an intrinsic motivation to learn and we must see some advantage to having engaged in the process (Knowles, Holton, & Swanson, 2005). The theory of andragogy revolves around the notion that as learners, we are individuals and our learning is purpose driven.

Andragogy is a way of learning that promotes freedom of thinking. There are no clear lines between the teacher and the learner. The student is a peer as well as a learner. Andragogy promotes a form of learning that is both voluntary and based on using prior knowledge to gain new knowledge.

Understanding what adults need to be successful learners helps the literacy coach working with the literacy leadership team in a number of ways: She or he is better able to plan appropriate agendas, to provide appropriate support, and to become a lead learner herself or himself.

How Andragogy Differs from Pedagogy

By contrast, the environment in which a young learner works from a pedagogical stance is characterized mostly by the transmission model of learning and instruction. The classroom for the young learner is highly structured and the curriculum content is produced and directed by the teacher. Lessons and assessment are the purview of the teacher, not the learner.

The word *pedagogy* itself comes from the Greek word *paid,* which means "child" and from *agogus,* which means "the leader of." One definition says that pedagogy is the art and science of learning and instruction with children. A pedagogical model is one that places the responsibility of learning with the school and/or teacher.

Historically, a pedagogical model promotes "group thinking" and education that has been described as "one size fits all." In most cases, rote learning is the approach, whereas with adult learners, active, participatory learning is encouraged. The learner depends on the teacher to dispense the information and there are clearly defined roles for the teacher and the learner.

A pedagogical model is one that assumes that the learner needs to learn only what the curriculum content asks the teacher to teach and does not assume that the learner needs to apply the information to his or her own life. Learning is *outside* of the learner. An andragogical model assumes that the learner has input into the curriculum content to be

TABLE 1.1

How Adult Learners Differ from Young Learners

Children	Adults
Need supervised practice	No need for direct supervision—learners are self-directed
Need repetitive practice	Limited need for repetitive practice
Learning how to learn	Learning for change/growth
Motivation comes from external stimuli	Motivation is from internal stimuli
Teacher helps children build and enlarge previously developed schema	Adults have enough schema to move forward to acquire new knowledge
Teacher helps children tap into prior knowledge to acquire new knowledge	Adults are self-motivated and can use prior knowledge to build new knowledge

learned and that it is very important what impact the learning will have on her or his life.

Although learners in a pedagogical model are considered a part of the process of learning, they are living through the experiences the teacher, the text, and the curriculum content have organized for them. A pedagogical model relies on the transmission of information to the learner; thus, lectures, assigned work, and prepared texts in other media are the foundations that support the model.

Finally, the young learner is motivated by extrinsic forces such as grades, parental approval, and in some cases even food. This is markedly different from the adult learner who is motivated by intrinsic factors such as self-satisfaction, self-approval or job satisfaction—although they are also motivated by some external factors such as monetary increases and job promotions. Table 1.1 summarizes some differences in the two groups.

Models of Adult Learning

We have addressed that adult learners are self-directed and learn by using their personal experiences. Andragogy is one model of adult learning, but there are others that can help clarify, support, and expand our understandings of working with colleagues. We will briefly review five theoretical models of adult learning that can serve literacy leadership teams in tackling adaptive challenges to bring about forward shifts in learning and instruction in schools: Cross's CAL Model, McClusky's Theory of Margin, Knox's Proficiency Theory, Jarvis's Learning Process, and Lave's Theory of Situational Learning. Our descriptions are brief, since an elaborate explanation of each would certainly be beyond the scope and purpose of this book. Our hope is that we will provide you with enough information for you to use and to whet your appetite to investigate each theory further if needed.

Cross's CAL Model

Cross's model of characteristics of adults as learners (CAL) focuses not only on what adults need to learn but also how they learn. She believes that adult learners are characterized by either personal characteristics or situational characteristics. Personal characteristics would be those that have to do with our physical, psychological, and sociocultural conditions. They would include such things as getting older, going through developmental stages, and moving from our parents' home to our own home. Situational characteristics are those that are completely separate from the personal and constitute our ability to choose to learn as opposed to "having" to learn and our ability to decide how much learning we are going to attend to at any given time (Cross, 1981). Unlike children, adults can make choices about where to live and where to go to school.

McClusky's Theory of Margin

In a 1963 publication McCluskey discussed this theory of adult learners as those who can balance the internal and external factors that are given to them. We seek this balance between the "energy needed and the amount available," and this is seen as life's "load." In addition, we have personal "power" that gives us the ability to deal with the load. What energy we have left is thought of as the "margin in life."

For us to engage in a process of learning, we must have some "margin of power" (McClusky, 1970). We need to be able to handle a variety of situations and responsibilities—often simultaneously. This ability to change and adapt to different life events distinguishes us from younger learners.

Knox's Proficiency Theory

As adults, we are motivated to learn by different stimuli. Often these motivations, as stated earlier, are intrinsic. There is some expectation that as adults, we will be highly capable to engage in a number of roles. This capability Knox thought of as "proficiency" to achieve. Knox believes that we are able to perform "satisfactorily" if we are given the opportunity (Knox, 1980). Key elements of this model are performance, aspiration, self, general and specific environments, discrepancies, learning activity, and the teacher's role (Merriam & Cafferella, 1999). This theory of learning is based on the learner's motivation to learn, and it assumes that he or she will be able to learn at a proficient level.

Jarvis's Learning Process

As teachers, we know that children need to be able to assemble a schematic working system to be able to learn. Experiences are crucial for newer and broader schema to be created. We know that when students lack these experiences, academic learning is difficult or impossible. Jarvis (1987) believes that *all* learning is based on experiences. This learning occurs in a social situation and can take any of nine different pathways, three of which do not lead to learning (presumption, non-consideration, and rejection) and six of which do (preconscious, practice, memorization, contemplation, reflective practice, and experimental). Merriam and Cafferella (1999) see these as a hierarchy of learning: The first three are nonlearning platforms, the second three are nonreflective learning platforms, and the final three are self-reflective platforms. The last are also higher levels of learning (Jarvis, 1987).

Lave's Theory of Situational Learning

Unlike the kinds of learning we do in the classroom, ones that require learning out of "context," Lave (1988) suggests that there are learning activities that can be "situational." This type of learning is based on a community setting, and occurs in a social environment. Situational learning is characterized by collaborative social interaction and requires that information be presented in a relevant context. This applies to adult learners because they are more likely to have realistic problems that need to be resolved. Adult learners are expected to be critically reflective and to question their assumptions about answers to these problems (Stein, 1998). Although we don't see this as strictly the purview of the adult classroom and we do encourage the community of learning philosophy, we think that adult learners are more inclined to take on these types of learning experiences without direction from a teacher.

   Young (1993) believes that there are four distinct components that should be included in this type of learning: situations that promote realistic, problem-centered and complex activities; situations where teachers must scaffold the learners; situations where teachers must be seen as learning facilitators, not transmitters of information; and an ongoing assessment to determine how the learner and the learning community are progressing (Stein, 1998).

Although each theory supports and overlaps, it is under this situational learning orientation that we see the literacy leadership teams functioning to support forward shifts in learning and instruction. Members of the literacy leadership team will engage in realistic solution seeking—searching for answers that are centered on the strengths and needs of the school. Members will develop new knowledge based on their experiences in the school environment and their relationship with members of the total learning environment.

Who Is an Adult Learner?

When does a pedagogical model of learning become less effective and an andragogical model more effective? Who is considered the "adult" learner? According to Knowles, Holton, and Swanson (2005), there are several things to be considered: the biological, the psychological, the social, and the legal aspects.

The biological features to be considered are physical maturation, whereas the legal age of adulthood is determined legislatively. Socially, we are considered adults when we begin to work outside of the home or take on adult roles such as parent and spouse. Psychological adulthood happens when we develop a sense of self and we take responsibility for our own lives. As learners, it is this last one that has the most meaning.

In truth, however, becoming an adult does not happen linearly but rather by stages. People may take on some features of adulthood when they are in their early teens but still maintain a "pedagogical" stance with regard to schooling. Most people, however, will become adults when they take on the responsibility of living on their own and creating their own families.

Summary

In this chapter, we briefly reviewed the differences between young learners and adult learners and what theorists think is involved for adult learners to be successful. The concept of andragogy is a vital foundation to support literacy leadership teams over time in working with their colleagues at school. This information is important for literacy leadership teams because when teams are successful and productive, they recognize that adults have significantly different learning orientations than young learners. Adults are motivated by different life events that occur at both the social as well as biological levels.

In Chapter 2, we will examine the conditions for learning that should be in place at the school to support professional learning and in the classroom to promote student learning. Based on the work of Brian Cambourne's *conditions of learning* (1988), we will discuss and illustrate how these conditions can scaffold and encourage forward shifts in learning and instruction.

LIBRETTO

As the middle school literacy coach, Eva has been asked to put together a literacy leadership team to study the needs of the school. She has determined, through various conversations with faculty members, that faculty sees the school's needs very differently. Additionally, she notices that many faculty members don't want to be involved in resolving any of the issues the principal sees as significant. Because her charge from the principal is narrowly defined and quite specific, Eva knows that she is faced with a daunting challenge. She needs to include faculty members that aren't on the same page with her or the principal. She decides that she will focus her efforts on getting this group to join the team first.

Eva identifies three teachers who have been particularly hard to approach—one language arts, one social studies, and one science teacher—and she makes an appointment to talk with them. When they get together after school the following week, this is what transpires.

"Hi everyone, Eva begins, "I'm so glad that you agreed to talk with me. I really need some help with this problem the principal has given me to solve. We have been asked to form a literacy leadership team and address the needs of the school. I know that we all have different opinions about this, so I wanted to get your input and try to determine which are the most crucial issues. Then we can prioritize them and when we meet with all the other team members we will have a good first start."

Each teacher gives his or her opinion. Mrs. Jones says that she needs more help with her struggling readers and her English language learners. Mr. Gaines replies that as the social studies teacher, he needs more appropriate materials, and Mr. Franks only wants his class to run more smoothly.

Eva asks Mr. Gaines and Mr. Franks why they need these things. They pause for a minute and then Mr. Franks says, "It's the kids in my classroom. They aren't motivated, they don't listen, and they can't pay attention for five minutes at a time."

Eva responds, "Why is that do you think?"

"Because, they have low reading scores, and the materials are too difficult," he replies. "That's exactly right," says Mr. Gaines, "that's what's wrong in my classroom too."

"So, I guess all three of you really are talking about the same situation. You all need help with students who are struggling readers, whether they are first or second language learners." They all nod in agreement.

"So, do you think if we form this team that we can find a way to address this concern that you all seem to share?" Eva tells the three teachers that she thinks they will be able to study issues and find information that they can use to make these critical changes in their classrooms. They agree to join the team, and Eva tells them that she will be in touch with them soon about the time and place for the first meeting.

Reflections

1. What instructional practices from adult learning theory did Eva use to help motivate these adult learners to join her cause?

2. How can she use these instructional practices to further the understanding of the entire team?

3. What concepts of situational learning did she utilize and why was this effective?

Exchange

You have read at the beginning of this chapter the scenario about the faculty meeting and you probably have suggestions for exchanging the negative atmosphere for a positive one. What did you find in the chapter that helps you better understand adult learners that could have made the faculty meeting more productive for all the members? What could Ms. Jarrod have done to create a feeling that the faculty was valued as individuals? If you were the literacy coach responsible for setting up the literacy leadership team, what would you say to the principal before the meeting so that this situation does not occur?

Chapter 2

Understanding Conditions for Learning

"X-ed" Change

James was new to the school and was being asked to take on the role of the literacy coach. His first task was to form a literacy leadership team with one member from each of the content areas. He decided that in the interest of time, he would just appoint someone from each area and send an email to the appointees, telling them that he wanted them to work with him on the team. He set the time and date for the first meeting and started to prepare his materials. The day of the meeting arrived and James gathered his things and waited in the media center. Some of the team members showed up and some didn't. The principal was conspicuously absent.

James: Well, thanks to the four of you who came this afternoon. Let's start by going around the table and giving your name and subject area.

Mr. Quinn: I'm Bob Quinn and I teach English. I have no idea why we are here, but I want to be a team player, so I'm here.

Mrs. Brown: I'm Dorothy Brown and I teach AP math. I heard earlier from the principal that this was going to be a year-long course on solving school issues, so I'm glad to be here, too.

Ms. Randall: Hi, I'm Jennie Randall and I teach vo-tech. I think I was picked because I'm new and need a committee assignment.

Mr. Roberts: Hi, I'm Rob Roberts and I teach music—band really. I hope you can tell me what kind of time commitment this is going to take, because you know how busy the fall is with football games and the two required concerts. Thanks.

James: Thanks, everyone. I'm James Ogilvey and I have been asked to form this leadership team with members from each of the content areas as well as counseling and administration. I see that there are several members who couldn't make it today. We will just proceed and perhaps they will show up later. If not, I will prepare a report of what we accomplished today and send it along to them as well as to each of you.

For today, I would like to explore issues that you think are ones that need closer scrutiny here at McGovern High. I have prepared a list of the ones that I think should be our top priorities. Please look it over and rank-order them as to how important you think they are and we will begin discussing each one.

The meeting continued along for another 30 minutes with the team members still uncertain why they were really there, where these meetings were going, what their roles were. After the hour was up, James had developed a flowchart of the pertinent issues that had been discussed. He thanked the members for coming and told them that he would send them the summary later on by email with the time and date of the next meeting.

After reading this chapter on the conditions for learning, review the Exchange questions at the end of the chapter and discuss with your team members what changes you would make so that this team could be successful.

By considering the conditions for learning as a literacy leadership team, the team can then begin to look at the place where most instruction takes place—the classroom. We believe that these conditions can form a solid foundation for the literacy leadership team.

To assist the team's understanding of Cambourne's conditions of learning and how they apply to the school and classroom, the next few paragraphs will go into brief but detailed accounts of each condition. Keep in mind that there is no specific order for the conditions since, when learning is taking place, they occur simultaneously. Also keep in mind that the conditions for learning should not be developed into a checklist of classroom activities but rather a "synergistic network" (Cambourne, 2007) or framework for thinking about learning and instruction.

As adults, we know that we are motivated to learn information for a variety of reasons, not the least of which is self-improvement. Generally speaking, adult learners are self-regulating and self-directed in a solution-seeking learning environment (Knowles, 1978). Because literacy leadership teams are comprised of adult learners, we will explore how the work of Brian Cambourne (1988) is applicable to school for teachers and students, and how this knowledge can be used when considering issues at a school to improve learning and instruction. Cambourne's work can assist us in identifying an initial adaptive challenge and may guide us in a specific direction to investigate further.

Conditions for Learning

Brian Cambourne (1988) concluded that there are eight universal conditions of complex learning that are in place during language acquisition. Although his work is originally on the conditions *of* learning, we refer to them as conditions *for* learning from a teacher's perspective and use them as a guide to create supportive learning environments in school. The conditions of learning that Cambourne found are demonstration, responsibility, approximation, response, immersion, expectation, engagement, and use/employment. Although these eight conditions occur concurrently, we will address each one individually with the understanding that optimal learning exists when all of them are in place in what Cambourne refers to as a "synergistic network." Additionally, Cambourne (2007) currently places the condition of engagement at the core of learning.

It has been our experience that engagement progresses within the learner's *zone of proximal development* (Vygotsky, 1978). Extrapolating from the work of Tharp and Gallimore (1988), we feel that within the condition of engagement there are four levels taking learners from subject-centered learning to solution-seeking learning with complex sublevels existing within each. As a framework for thinking when learning is taking place, the first level of engagement appears to exist at a social plane with interaction among learners and more knowledgeable others. At the second level of engagement, learners are consciously self-regulating. As the learner progresses through the levels of engagement that we have identified, the learning behavior becomes "fossilized" (Vygotsky, 1978), or automatic. The fourth level of engagement occurs when the learner comes to the understanding of what he or she has learned and what he or she doesn't know. The fourth level is where learning is recursive and the learner returns to the first level with new learning occurring while deepening understanding.

Demonstration

Although each condition is dependent and builds on one another, the condition of demonstration is one that nearly every single person refers to as one manner of learning something. Ask any group of adults how they learned something and nearly everyone will mention that they observed someone involved in what they attempted to learn. For example, think about how you learned to ride a bicycle, drive a car, knit, or skate. In almost every situation, we observed someone engaged in the activity that made it look simple—so simple that we felt we could learn to do it too.

Through multiple exposures to an activity, we not only developed a sense that we could accomplish the activity, but we also began to understand the benefit of engaging in the activity. Perhaps the benefit is for entertainment, to further another activity, to support a sense of independence, or to assist us in helping others, to mention a few. Let's take driving a car, for example. After many demonstrations in the society we live in, driving a car provides us with the independence to go to the theater and the grocery store, or to visit relatives and friends. All of these activities are what Cambourne (1988) refers to as contextually relevant. Additionally, he reminds us that demonstrations have to be continuously repeated and that there is no designated length of time that these should take place. These two caveats should have a tremendous impact on the function of a literacy coach and the literacy leadership team. Once again, by taking a look at ourselves first, we will realize that the demonstrations that we observed were always demonstrations of an entire or whole activity. Shifting gears, turning on the windshield wipers, or braking, by themselves, were never demonstrated as isolated activities but rather as functions of the entire or whole concept of driving a car. This concept should have incredible impact on the function of a literacy coach and literacy leadership team in supporting schools in making forward shifts.

What impact does understanding the importance of demonstration have on the literacy coach and the literacy leadership team? In our work with literacy coaches and literacy leadership teams, we have found that both the coach and the team need to be able to reflect and investigate what demonstrations are being provided in school. Many times, unconscious demonstrations are provided that are counterproductive to our intentions. An example that comes to mind is the idea that assessment should guide instruction. Yet, often literacy coaches and literacy leadership teams will ask classroom teachers to engage in a specific instructional practice without first considering assessment, and in the same breath say that teachers need to use assessment to guide instruction. The same would be true of a literacy coach providing an observation lesson without understanding the students' strengths and needs.

Responsibility

Literacy coaches and literacy leadership teams should be viewed as "lead-learners" by showing students and teachers that they accept full responsibility for their learning. Both literacy coaches and literacy leadership teams need to show that they are self-regulating and self-directed. The condition of responsibility in learning highlights the importance of the learner being in the metaphorical driver's seat. No one can learn *for* someone else, but everyone can learn *from* someone else. The condition of responsibility in learning manifests itself when learners are willing to make decisions about their learning and more knowledgeable others trust that learners will be involved in the demonstrations provided.

Although certainly not an exhaustive list, there are some behaviors that promote responsibility in learning. Responsibility is encouraged in classrooms and schools when learners are asked to try something before asking for help. Furthermore, when help is required it is offered in a collaborative solution-seeking spirit. Schools and classrooms that offer choice in an information-intensive learning environment are encouraging learners to take responsibility for their learning and are promoting self-efficacy (Bandura, 1998).

It is a primary responsibility of a literacy coach and literacy leadership team to constantly be checking themselves so that team decisions are generated by collaborative solution seeking rather than didactic decision making. Didactic decision making removes the element of responsibility from the learner and places it on the teacher or more knowledgeable other.

Approximation

Most teachers and parents are familiar with approximation as a condition for learning. The infant who begins to coo and make sounds is approximating the oral language she or he is exposed to through multiple demonstrations provided by siblings, other children, and adults. The kindergartner who mimics writing letters by making squiggles on paper is approximating writing based on many demonstrations he or she has encountered. Many of us have encountered young children who approximate reading a story by holding a book and pretending (or approximating) to read. As adult learners, when we predict and estimate, we're approximating an outcome based on our current level of knowledge.

Cambourne (1988) tells us that when people think of learning as a form of hypothesis testing, approximations are paramount for processing information. Moreover, approximations are necessary for learners to develop a feedforward mechanism that functions to make learning efficient (Johnston, 1997). A feed-forward mechanism is our ability to predict and anticipate. Approximations are predictions and estimations that initiate information processing. Without approximations, information processing is halted and sophisticated processing becomes an impossibility. Consequently, schools and classrooms should be set up for learners to feel free to approximate in order to jump-start information processing.

Part of a literacy coach's and literacy leadership team's charge is to ensure that the school is set for all learners (children and adults) to approximate, learn, and grow. Setting up an environment where learners are free to take risks is critical. Notice we did not say "risk-free" since all learning requires a certain level of risk. Without approximations being accepted, the likelihood of forward shifts in learning will not occur. We have to accept that making mistakes is part of learning. All learners will make mistakes in their learning, and this includes teachers who will make mistakes in implementing instructional practices.

Response

Learning does not take place in a vacuum. Most learning is accompanied or prompted by responses from others during the process of learning. In Cambourne's (1988) work, the term *response* is used rather than the mechanistic term *feedback*. Feedback generally indicates a one-sided point of view irrelevant of the learner. Historically, education has focused on providing corrective feedback. In providing "corrective" feedback, we are diminishing the importance of approximations and taking the responsibility of learning from the learner. However, by providing a generative response, we are honoring and extending the learner's approximations to encourage forward shifts and the development of a self-extending system (Clay, 2001).

We think of feedback as a component of a transmission model of learning that focuses on memorization of content, and we see response as a transformational model of learning that promotes critical forward thinking. It will be up to the team to weigh the benefits of feedback and response in relation to the identified adaptive challenge. Responses in learning are based on the balance between the learner and the more knowledgeable other. Providing a response is dependent on the learner's experiences and the experiences of the more knowledgeable other to promote independence. A response is generally made respectfully and sensitively to a learner's approximations.

The issue of response is critical for literacy coaches and literacy leadership teams to promote forward thinking with children and adults. Commonly, responses at school focus on acknowledging, celebrating, or collaboratively seeking solutions based on a demonstration provided by either students or teachers. In other words, most responses fall into three broad categories. They focus on a knowledge or skill level, stretching the learner's understanding, or guiding toward a specific resource.

Immersion

When we were learning to speak, we were surrounded by oral language regardless of the heritage language spoken at home. From the day we were born, we were immersed in oral language with people talking to us, about us, and around us. Consequently, because we were immersed in this oral language, learning to speak was facilitated.

Taking our cue from oral language acquisition, we need to immerse our students and teachers in an information-intensive environment where reading, writing, speaking, listening, and viewing are relevant, meaningful, and thoughtful. By immersing everyone in an information-intensive environment, we're acknowledging, utilizing, and appreciating the available technology that our students are growing and comfortable with in their everyday lives.

In addressing immersion as a condition for learning, we prefer to use the term *information-intensive environment* rather than the popularly used *print-rich* or *literacy-rich* environment. It seems to us that in order to prepare students for a biotechnical age, print alone will not be enough. The task of the literacy coach and the literacy leadership team is to consider and plan how to create this information-intensive environment where all involved will benefit. At the classroom level, creating an information-intensive environment means providing on-line and off-line materials for students. In elementary classrooms (pre-K–5), this might include workboards, word walls/theme charts, computers, books (narrative and nonnarrative), dictionaries, and thesauruses. In secondary classrooms (6–12), an information-intensive environment may include content area textbooks, word theme charts, computers, books (narrative and nonnarrative), primary sources, and reference materials. We separate the grade levels to highlight the impact of creating an information-intensive environment, and how we can adjust the learning environment to better meet the needs of all learners.

At the school level, consideration needs to be given to how the school is creating an information-intensive environment for everyone involved. Immersion at the school level investigates updating technology, community involvement, providing professional magazines and books across content areas, looking at professional learning opportunities, and creating an environment where everyone feels safe to take risks.

Expectation

Expectation needs to be considered from the perspective of students, teachers, the literacy coach, the literacy leadership team, and the principal. If the expectation among all involved in a school is not congruent, forward shifts will not happen. Rosenthal and Jacobson (1968) addressed the importance of expectation in learning. Additionally, expectation is correlated to self-esteem in learners (Cambourne, 1988) and self-efficacy (Bandura, 1998). The idea of truly knowing students and colleagues supports our notion of what we expect. Consequently, our expectations have a powerful influence on learners' emotions, learning, and memory when they process information (Rushton, Eitelgeorge, & Zickafoose, 2003), provided we assess and reflect on the learners' strengths and needs.

When our expectations are too low, poor attitudes and apathy are likely to be manifested in learners. Experienced teachers know that these emotions are counterproductive to learning. When our expectations are too high, learners may develop a defeatist attitude prompted by assignments and projects that are too difficult to accomplish. Once again, these emotions are counterproductive to learning. Therefore, striking a perfect balance of expectations becomes a critical point for consideration for teachers, literacy coaches, and literacy leadership teams when we consider that emotions are generally accepted as a gateway to long-term memory (Caine & Caine, 1994).

Engagement

A crucial condition for learning is what Smith (1981) calls "engagement." Cambourne (1988) found that there are four principles for true engagement to take place. The first principle is that learners believe that if they delve into a learning situation, they will be successful. Think of it this way: Would you attempt to do something that you knew for a fact you would fail? This principle highlights the point that one factor that needs to be in place for learners to be engaged is the idea that if they attempt to do something, they expect to be successful. There has to be a sense of self-efficacy in place to be engaged (Bandura, 1998). No one wants to attempt something at which he or she will fail.

The literacy leadership team, with the guidance of an effective and efficient literacy coach, should always keep this expectation in mind when executing a plan that will directly impact students and teachers. Particularly, teachers need to feel that if they implement a new instructional practice, they will be successful in promoting learning in their classrooms.

Understanding the purpose and the benefit in an activity or learning situation is a second principle identified by Cambourne. It's having the understanding of "what's-in-it-for-me." Without this sense of purpose or clear understanding of benefits, learners are not likely to be engaged. Hence, it's up to the literacy leadership team to ensure that students and teachers understand the importance of acquiring high levels of multiple literacies.

Cambourne's third principle of engagement is the idea that if someone attempts to learn something, there will not be any negative impact during the process of learning. In other words, to ensure engagement by a learner, the learner needs to feel safe to take risks. When a literacy coach coaches or when a literacy leadership team attempts to implement a schoolwide plan, consideration should be given to ensure that all involved understand that everyone is safe to take risks in attempting a new instructional practice or supporting the implementation of a school-wide program.

The fourth principle of engagement, according to Cambourne, is the concept that the learner respects and admires the person providing the demonstrations. This guiding principle is highlighted in *The Literacy Coach: Guiding in the Right Direction* (Puig & Froelich, 2007), when it is repeatedly stated that for literacy coaches to acquire credibility they need to teach students on a daily basis (Puig & Froelich, 2007; Casey, 2006). It has been our experience that by teaching students on a daily basis, we acquire the respect and admiration of our colleagues, which in turn increases the likelihood of colleagues being engaged in collaborative solution seeking within the literacy leadership team and the literacy coach. Think of your own teaching experiences. The students who were usually engaged during your demonstrations were the ones that respected and admired you, not necessarily as a teacher but as a person.

Cambourne's four principles of engagement are key points to consider as a literacy leadership team to ensure that all participants are engaged in all demonstrations. These principles should prompt the team to think that learners need to be convinced that they are liked and respected, special attention should be given to the kinds of demonstrations provided, and a certain level of awareness of the principles of engagement should be in place.

Use/Employment

Research in neuroscience tells us that practice assists us in taking information into long-term memory (Jensen, 1998; Wolfe, 2001). The concept of use is not new in education. We have all grown up in school with use or practice incorporated into nearly all aspects of our schooling. Although not necessarily the most effective instructional practice, many of us remember writing spelling words over and over, or memorizing multiplication facts by repeating them to ourselves or to a classmate—committing the information into long-term memory for further use in the future in other learning enterprises.

Taking into account the concept of use, we believe that effective instructional practices couple use or practice with social interaction in order for new learning to take place. Cambourne has stated that new learning is a by-product of social interaction and personal reflection. This concept is further validated by Vygotsky (1978) and Caine and Caine (1994) when they claim that learning is amplified through socialization with others.

Adult Learners and Cambourne's Conditions

We have shown how Cambourne's concepts apply to young learners. But how do they fit with the adult learner? Table 2.1 shows what we believe the connections are.

As you can see, some of the conditions, such as use/employment, approximation, and immersion, fit the same way for adults as they do for younger learners. Some of the others require the learner be more self-regulated. Responsibility is a good example of this. This is important to the literacy leadership team leader as well as to the members that will be working with their colleagues to think about as they plan for meetings. The team leader needs to consider that when we want to learn new information, we need to have multiple opportunities to engage in the process—to see how it is done, to practice it ourselves, and to take ownership over it, much the same way a younger learner would.

Summary

In this chapter we reviewed the work of Brian Cambourne and the conditions of learning as they apply to school and classrooms. Over time, the eight conditions that Cambourne proposes as condition of learning directly apply as conditions for learning to impact how a literacy leadership team, with the support of a literacy coach, can use the information to guide the team as they tackle adaptive challenges and develop a long-term plan of execution to improve instruction. Based on our experience, when planning, literacy leadership teams need to keep Cambourne's eight conditions (demonstration, responsibility, approximation, response, immersion, expectation, engagement, use/employment) at the forefront of their thinking with special attention given to the four principles of engagement.

TABLE 2.1

What We Need to Learn

Child	Adult
Strong demonstrations: Child needs to see someone do the things that they want us to learn.	Strong demonstrations: Even for adults it is important that there are strong models, especially when learning in unknown domains.
Use/employment: Child needs time to practice what we want to learn.	Use/employment: Few of us learn something the first time. Practice is essential.
Response: Child needs to know how she is doing and when she is not doing so well. Appropriate response is essential.	Response: Giving adult learners appropriate response helps them make necessary adjustments.
Immersion: Research shows that when we are immersed in the process of learning, it is easier to learn.	Immersion: Though not as essential as for children, a variety of items help adults learn.
Expectations: Teacher builds a sense of expectation for the child.	Expectations: These are self-directed.
Responsibility: Teacher and student are both responsible for learning.	Responsibility: Adults take responsibility for learning.
Approximation: It is important that we be allowed to make mistakes and to learn from them.	Approximation: Not getting it right the first time should be okay.
Engagement: The learner needs to be motivated to learn, and when they are there will be engagement.	Engagement: Adult learners learn best when they have a vested interest in what they are learning, and thus are engaged.

Karin wanted to be able to work in the classrooms as well as work with her colleagues as the literacy coach. She hoped to help form a strong leadership team and help the school meet its educational goals. She studied the school mission statement, reviewed the assessment program, and reviewed past test scores. She read all of the reports that the school had published on the makeup of the student body, and she talked with teachers individually about their perceptions of where the school was headed. She still did not have a strong feeling for the kinds of things she should focus on. Karin thought that perhaps her problem was that she did not have a plan of action herself—maybe she wasn't self-directed enough.

Karin decided that she would make a list of things that she could do to help in the classrooms she was assigned to and have the teachers check off the ones they wanted her to pursue. She also made a note to talk about this during the next literacy leadership team meeting so that the classroom teachers could see how she was seeking solutions for critical issues and the ways in which she was processing information.

Reflections

1. In what ways was Karin employing the conditions for learning?

2. In what ways was Karin not employing the conditions for learning?

3. If you were the literacy coordinator, how could you help Karin develop a plan that was consistent with the goals of the school, the teachers, and the students as well as follow the principles of literacy coaching?

Exchange

You have read the "'X-ed' Change" as well as the chapter and the libretto. Revisit James's dilemma and decide where you would make appropriate changes so that the team members are inside the decision-making process. Which of the conditions for learning do you think were in place and which ones weren't? Which ones weren't vital to success? Why or why not?

Chapter 3

Developing a Common Language

"X-ed" Change

Barbara started her team meeting by addressing each member personally. She then proceeded to launch into the agenda.

"Thanks for coming everyone. As you know, we are being challenged to build consensus here at the school by addressing the stipulated issues that the county office has recognized as strategic for this school year. We will be examining the literacy components used in your classrooms and giving corrective feedback for restructuring our direct instruction procedures. We want to think through the issues of how we talk about and instruct our struggling students as well as our English as second language learners. Our charge is to redefine our literacy centers as places for optimal expansion. The reading and writing processes that have been promoted will be examined and new efforts to enhance primary, secondary, and tertiary attributes will be developed. Does anyone have any questions so far? If you have any suggestions for ways we can reach our mandate, I would appreciate it if you would type them up and place them in my mailbox by the end of the week."

Barbara, without really knowing it, has set artificial walls around her ability to lead the team. Read the chapter on developing a common language and the libretto at the end. Discuss what changes you would make to Barbara's introduction. Rewrite it so that it capitalizes on what you learned from the chapter.

As we can see from the preceding scenario, Barbara may be creating a situation with her literacy leadership team that will prevent them from being successful or sustaining change. In situations where disparate groups try to conceptualize new or unknown factors, it is advisable first to establish the ground rules by which they will all operate. One component of this is to establish a common vocabulary—a common language.

In working with many literacy leadership teams, it has been our experience that in order for the team to get started on the right foot, a common language has to be developed. Overall, language can be ambiguous and vague. Compound that with a group of adults with a variety of experiences attempting to interpret school data, and the result has the potential to be disastrous. Consequently, we cannot overstate the importance of developing a common language as a first step to minimize misinterpretation and to guide a school in a state of transition.

To assist literacy leadership teams in developing a common language, talking about and dissecting the benefits and features is a critical step, since essentially it will be the responsibility of the literacy leadership team to share and update the faculty's language to promote forward shifts. In particular, understanding the benefits of any enterprise, such as developing a common language, is one of the principles Cambourne (1988) describes as essential to increase the likelihood of engagement. A prime conduit and support for the team to develop a common language is the literacy coach (Puig & Froelich, 2007). The important role of the literacy coach in supporting the literacy leadership team cannot be overemphasized.

Benefits of Developing a Common Language

Do you remember the first time you heard the term *google* or *blog*? Do you remember what you thought they meant? Can you remember a meeting that you attended where the person (much like Barbara in the "'X-ed' Change" scenario) assumed you had a level of understanding that perhaps you didn't? We have all been in a learning situation that required us to learn a new lexicon or vocabulary. Similarly, we have all had classes in which we were asked to understand terms and concepts that were foreign to us. As adults, we have the requisite skills and strategic knowledge to be able to figure out what to do.

One of the important aspects of team building is to start by developing a common language. Ideally, we all need to think about and respond to terms with the same level of understanding in order to understand each others' interpretations. We have found that if this doesn't happen, team members will very likely not engage at the level needed to make appropriate changes and promote improved instructional practices. Hence, some of the benefits for developing a common language as a literacy leadership team are:

1. Improves communication and better interpretation of data
2. Expands thinking by applying new concepts to known words
3. Economizes on time when meeting to discuss adaptive challenges
4. Develops a sense of community
5. Creates a safe environment

By developing a common language among the literacy coach and the literacy leadership team members, communication is improved. This increases the likelihood that when the literacy leadership team begins to identify an initial adaptive challenge, they will be closer to the true issue at hand. By having a common language among members, the dynamics of the team will be more powerful in determining an initial adaptive challenge, interpreting the data, and investigating a menu of solutions. This would be virtually impossible without a common language. A literacy leadership team without a common language, as in any team, is equivalent to a country running itself with all its citizens not having a common language.

Features of Developing a Common Language

We've discussed the issue of benefits—the "why" and its application to the literacy leadership team through the lens of engagement as a condition for learning. Since we understand the benefit to the team, we also need to address the features—the "what"—of developing a common language. When we talk about the features of a common language, we believe that there are five critical attributes that surface to facilitate productive conversations among members. The five features of developing a common language that serve to sustain and expand our conversations are:

1. Relationships among words and concepts
2. Transferability of definitions
3. Utilization of language in a self-improving system
4. Solidification of concepts
5. Unification of parts to a whole

Relationships among Words and Concepts

When we think about the concept of vocabulary development, we are look-ing at four kinds of relationship between words and concepts (Alvermann, Phelps, & Ridgeway, 2007). The first of these is having a known word and a known concept. For example, literacy coaches know the term *schemata* and we know that it means having *prior knowledge* about a topic. For some literacy leadership team members this might be an unknown word (schemata) but a known concept (prior knowledge). This is the second relationship. The third relationship is a known word but an unknown concept. Some team members might also know the term *schemata* (known word) but not that it has anything to do with *prior knowledge* (unknown concept). The last relationship is an unknown word and an unknown concept. This would be the team members who have never heard of *schemata* and have no working knowledge of it.

The implications for the literacy leadership team are twofold. First, as we work toward developing a common language, we need to apply the four relationships we have just discussed to our instructional practices. We need to each work toward all members having words and concepts that are known to all. Second, it allows each team member to be able to say, without fear of recrimination, that he or she doesn't know a word or a concept. It implies that there are ways in which we think of literacy-specific language that some (or all) of us will not always have a universal answer to. On the surface these relationships seem like benefits (and might well be), but we see them as features of developing a common language so that the literacy leadership team can move forward with relevant issues.

Transferability of Definitions

Several features shape the development of a common language. The second feature we call *transferability*. This means that the language used from one area or domain can easily be redefined to meet those of another. For exam-ple, we use the word *strategies* extensively in education. This is one of those terms for which we all think we have a hard and fast definition. It is impor-tant to talk about what you as the literacy team leader mean and to hear from the team members what they think it means. For example, during an initial team meeting you might ask the members to brainstorm synonyms for *schema* and to come up with a working definition that is comfortable for everyone. In this way you can develop one common, working definition that everyone understands and can use without fear of misrepresentation.

Utilization of Language in a Self-Improving System

The third feature is that we have a self-improving system that we can draw on or utilize to improve our language development. This is a tool for thinking. When you develop a common language, you are activating this system (Clay, 2001). A self-improving system requires that you know what your limitations are, that you can make the appropriate modifications to fit the new parameters, and that you are motivated to make the necessary changes in your understandings of language so that consensus is reached among the team members.

Solidification of Concepts

The fourth important feature is that a common language "elicits, illuminates, and integrates" each team member's thinking (Shuler, 2002). We need to have a common understanding so that we can move toward our shared goals (Anderson, 1985). If one team member does not have the required working vocabulary that the rest of the team has, she or he probably won't be successful in her or his attempts to sustain change and will be resistant to team recommendations.

Unification of Experiences

The last feature is unification. When colleagues come from different content areas, as in the middle and high school settings, or even when they come from common teaching areas, as in elementary settings, everyone doesn't always see through the window exactly the same way. Our own personal experiences come to bear on our learning experiences just as our students do. We need to find common ground so that we can be unified in our attempts to develop lasting and meaningful change so that all students can benefit from the learning environment.

Specific Professional Learning Experiences for Developing a Common Language

The following professional learning opportunities are adapted from classroom instructional practices and are effective ways for the literacy leadership team to develop the common language necessary to serve as a springboard to expand school success. The professional learning practices we describe in the next few sections are activities that we have found to support powerful professional learning in developing a common language. Different literacy leadership team members may have additional practices that may be preferred by the team. We encourage the literacy coach and the literacy leadership team to experiment with these practices to find which will work best with the rest of the faculty.

FIGURE 3.1

Sample of Frayer Model

Definition (personal definition)	Characteristics
Process—a series of practices or methods that lead to the creation of knowledge	Steps, features, components, recursiveness, cognition, practice
Examples (from personal experiences)	**Nonexamples (from personal experiences)**
Learning to drive; learning to read; learning to write; etc.	Unknown

Prepared Vocabulary Study

This is a small group activity that a team leader sets up. She or he gives a group or groups a list of prepared terms on index cards and asks them first to consider what the terms mean to individuals and then to come to a group definition through their discussion. This can also be accomplished through such established vocabulary exercises such as concept maps (Schwartz, 1988) or the Frayer Model (Frayer, Frederick, & Klausmeier, 1969), which is a method of categorizing words. Using the Frayer Model to clarify the term *process,* it looks like Figure 3.1.

Another way to look at developing a common language would be by using a Semantic Feature Analysis (Baldwin, Ford, & Readance, 1981; Johnson & Pearson, 1984). This is a method of coming up with a definition by comparing a word's features to those of other terms in the same class or category. Using the term *assessment,* the Semantic Feature Analysis might look like Figure 3.2.

Self-Designed Vocabulary Study

These are exercises conducted in small groups that enable the team to decide which terminology is important to study and how to go about it. The group chooses several key terms that the members believe will be important to developing successful study group sessions throughout the school year. Different groups may choose different vocabulary.

In Table 3.1 on page 35 we have started a list of literacy terms that we think is a good place to begin when talking about developing a "collective" vocabulary to improve literacy learning and instruction. You can see that there are terms that have been used previously and the ones we feel

FIGURE 3.2
Semantic Feature Analysis

Assessment	Numerical	Observation	Norm-Referenced	Criterion-Referenced
Running record				
Tests				
Performance				
Writing Rubrics				

are more representative of present-day literacy instruction. The list is not exhaustive, and your team, because of the district or school they work in, may have different terms that they need to define.

Summary

This chapter provided information about the importance of developing a common language so that forward shifts can take place during the literacy leadership team meetings. If teams don't understand the complex terminology associated with literacy, there could be a breakdown in productivity of the team, leading to discouragement and no gains for the schools as well as the teachers. Additionally, in developing a common language, one powerful lesson we have learned is to steer away from acronyms and abbreviations. *Acronyms and abbreviations, although expedient, always have the potential for misinterpretations because they are always context associated.*

In Chapter 4, we will examine literacy processing and the importance of grounding our practice in theory. If the literacy leadership team does not understand the theoretical concepts associated with literacy as a process, they are likely to misinterpret data and ask teachers to implement inappropriate instructional practices (Clay, 2001; Gillion, 2004). Like developing a common language, understanding literacy processing is fundamental for literacy leadership teams.

TABLE 3.1

Common Terms

Current	Former
Information-intensive environment	Print-rich environment
Strategic activities or actions	Strategies
Workstations or learning stations	Centers
Reading as a process	The reading process
Writing as a process	The writing process
Nonnarrative text	Nonfiction text
Working systems	Cueing systems
Sources of information	Cues
Instructional practices	Instructional strategies
English language learner	Limited English proficient
Comprehensive literacy	Balanced literacy
Low-progress students	Struggling students
Book Talk	Picture Walk
Shocks of Awareness/Epiphanies	Ah-ha's
Alternative response	Incorrect response
Constructive/generative response	Corrective feedback
Student learning	Student achievement
Observation classroom	Model classroom
Temporary spelling	Invented spelling
Developing reader	Emergent reader
Professional learning	Professional development
Nontraditional learner	Learning disabled
Intentional instruction	Direct instruction
Personalized instruction	Individualized instruction
Facilitator in-service	Train the trainer
Adaptive challenge	Area of concern

Mark really liked his team members but felt a little out of place when they started talking about "strategies," "schema theory," and other theoretical aspects of learning and instruction that came along with his job. It wasn't that he didn't know what these terms meant—or at least he knew what his college textbooks said they meant—it was just that the literacy coach was using them in ways he hadn't heard of before, and the other team members seemed to understand exactly how he was using them. He was still trying to understand the concept of "intentional instruction" and why "direct" instruction was no longer acceptable. "Isn't all instruction intentional?" he thought to himself.

If Mark asked what each term meant, would his colleagues conclude that he was some kind of dunce and think that he shouldn't be teaching, much less on their team? He didn't want to wait to try to figure out how they were being used either. What should Mark do?

Reflections

1. What are at least two solutions Mark could use to resolve his dilemma?

2. What should the literacy coach know about Mark's dilemma that would help him out of his awkward situation?

3. As a colleague of Mark's, what could you do when terms come up that are commonly used?

4. In your team meetings, how would you address the need for mutual understanding?

Exchange

You've read the "'X-ed' Change" and determined that Barbara has gotten off to a rocky start. She has really set an impossible task for her team. Why? After reading the chapter, what are some ways in which Barbara could be more amenable to her team's "common language" needs? What could she have done before the meeting to help build a comfort zone for team members? What could you do to help the team members exchange their anxiety for confidence?

Chapter 4

Understanding Literacy Processing to Make Powerful Decisions

"X-ed" Change

Mary and Jackie met to discuss how they were going to address the parents at the next open house. They were selected to look at the current reading series and make recommendations as to whether the school should request a newer one, stay with the one they were currently using, or some combination. They had been doing some research about "published reading series" and really wanted the parents to support their choice with the administration. Bob, the literacy coach, overhearing their conversation, started to feel uneasy about the direction they were taking.

Mary: Jackie, I really like the reading series material we received from the publishers. I have thoroughly investigated it, and I believe we can make two- to three-year gains with most of our students. The other children probably can't make much progress anyway and will have to be referred.

Jackie: I know what you mean. I really liked the strong emphasis on phonics and vocabulary development. The worksheets have clear directions, and the examples are easy to understand. I don't think the cost is too excessive, but even so, if the parents back us up, then I don't think it will be a problem.

Bob: Hi Mary and Jackie. I couldn't help but overhear part of your conversation and I was wondering if you would talk to me about the overall qualities of this series. Could you tell me how it addresses literacy as a process and whether or not it looks at all the components students need to be successful?

Mary: Okay, Bob. I know you think we need one of those literature-based thing-a-ma-dos, but really, this series has a strong phonics section in each lesson as well as a list of vocabulary that goes along with the little stories. Each story has "response questions" at the end and there is even one of those little writing prompts to set the stage for reading the story.

Jackie: And don't forget, Mary, there is an assessment for each section and a final test at the end of each of the books. That is certainly a lot of stuff for the money and I think it will make the administration happy and I know the parents will love it when they see it.

Bob: Well, you know we are having a leadership team meeting the first of next week. Would you both promise me that you will attend to talk about this series with the other members? I think we all need to fully understand what we will be purchasing. I hope to see you then. (Bob leaves.)

Mary: Can you believe that guy? He thinks that the leadership team is going to change our minds. We have done our research and we know what we need to say about the new series. But maybe we should go so that we can convince them too.

Jackie: I think that is an excellent idea. After all, what do we have to lose?

Read the chapter, the libretto, and the reflection questions. Decide what Mary and Jackie can do to expand their knowledge of literacy as a process and working systems.

Interestingly, in our educational experiences, we often encounter educators that request less theory and more "strategies" (meaning instructional practices). Although we perfectly understand and respect our colleagues' requests for more instructional practices, we also understand that without the theoretical understanding of why we are doing something, we will never be able to defend our craft of learning and instruction. *All classroom activities reduced simply to a series of instructional practices without being grounded in theory will likely disappear or be replaced at the first sign of failure.* Consequently, when we implement instructional practices that are not grounded in theory, it is extremely difficult for anyone to defend and sustain the practice implemented, and it is difficult to enact change because we are unsure of why things aren't working successfully. Moreover, if we cannot defend and sustain any practice in education, we certainly will not be able to expand it.

Understanding literacy processing and how readers develop over time goes hand-in-hand with developing a common language. These concepts are the foundation on which literacy coaches and literacy leadership teams can sustain and expand success in school. We strongly feel that administrators, as well as published series of materials, can come and go, but *the conceptual understandings that educators have grounded in theory and supported by research can only be enhanced with change.*

Previously, we discussed the importance of developing a common language and we provided specific activities to promote the development of a common language from a collaborative solution-seeking perspective or andragogy. In this chapter we are going to address another tool to assist literacy leadership teams. With the support of a literacy coach, we will identify and refine an adaptive challenge or concern. We do this in order to pursue an appropriate line of alternative solutions so that we can better execute the solutions, while reflecting on how they are implemented.

Although volumes have been written on the developmental stages of reading acquisition and understanding literacy as a process, this chapter is not meant to answer all the important questions related to processing information, or the many issues that surround learning to read. This chapter is meant to help literacy leadership teams find practical information about such things as:

1. Knowing how readers develop over time
2. Understanding how we process information (reading, writing, speaking, listening, and viewing)
3. Assisting literacy leadership teams in developing a common language about literacy acquisition as a life-long process over time
4. Promoting dialogic conversations among colleagues as they seek solutions collaboratively

Standing on the shoulders of many educators (Clay, 2001; Pressley, 2002; Rosenblatt, 1994; and many others), we have come to a working definition of literacy. Although many definitions exist, we define *literacy* as an overt act of engagement involving, singly or in combination, viewing, listening, speaking, writing, and reading. Hence, understanding literacy as a process is understanding how learners—all learners—process information by viewing, listening, speaking, writing, and reading. Ideally, the literacy leadership team, with the support of a knowledgeable literacy coach, should define literacy in their own words in order to sustain and expand school success. The conversations generated in defining literacy will strengthen the literacy leadership team's ability to defend necessary changes in order to sustain and expand success. Based on our understanding of the literature and personal experiences in teaching, the next sections of this chapter will address reading and writing and the reciprocity that they have to each other.

Reading as a Process

It is important to point out that we say reading *is a process* and not *the reading process*. By addressing it as "the reading process," we are implying that there is a single process. Conventional wisdom, along with years of experience in education, has shown us that there is no single process that is identical to someone else's when reading. This is a critical point for a literacy leadership team to understand when involved in developing a common language. Throughout this book, you'll notice key areas where we need to develop a common language. Once again, we need this common language so we can understand literacy as a process and its impact on analyzing data. In this way, we will be better able to make powerfully informed decisions for our schools.

We are going to temporarily break up the complex act of literacy processing so we can talk about the different working systems to use when processing information. Afterward, those working systems will be reassembled into what we generally refer to as *the act of reading*. Although there are many metacognitive working systems, contemporary literature addresses six broad categories of cognitive working systems: the graphophonic working system, the schematic working system, the semantic working system, the pragmatic working system, the lexical working system, and the syntactic working system. In the next few paragraphs, we'll explain each working system individually and then move on to how these working systems impact the reciprocal act of processing in writing (Clay, 2001; Fountas & Pinnell, 2006).

The Graphophonic Working System

The graphophonic working system is the working knowledge of sounds and the symbols associated with them. Your graphophonic working system is what assists you in decoding printed words at multiple levels or strata simultaneously. Generally, bilingual learners have two graphophonic working systems, trilingual learners have three, and so on. Monolinguals from different parts of a country might have a different graphophonic working system than a contemporary from another part of the same country. A native Bostonian, for example, certainly uses a different sound system than a native southerner might use.

For most of us, we know the graphophonic system is working when we listen to students read and think about the reader's knowledge of letters and sounds. Regardless of whether the reader is a first-grader or a senior in high school, all readers rely on the graphophonic working system when constructing meaning from print. They do this in conjunction with other language working systems. When readers rely solely on the graphophonic working system, they become handicapped in developing a defensible interpretation of what they are reading. For example, if a student relies solely on the graphophonic working system, it will not help her or him when reading identically looking words that have different pronunciations or definitions. Take the word *refuse*. Depending on how one pronounces it, it can mean not wanting to do something or garbage. In order to know how to pronounce it, a reader needs to bring in other working systems to construct meaning.

To understand the assembling of sounds and letters as a graphophonic working system while observing a reader, a teacher needs to reflect and question what awareness the reader has of the relationship between sounds and letters. *Only by questioning and reflecting can teachers support students in developing as literate individuals.*

The Schematic Working System

The schematic working system consists of all the background knowledge and prior experiences that one brings to all literate enterprises. Your schematic working system enables you to anticipate and predict how a story might end and why. It enables you to comprehend a concept by adding to your understanding of a scheme. The schematic working system is what keeps you on the edge of your seat in the theater or craving for more after finishing a great book. It is this working system that aids you in reading into and beyond a text. Critical thinking cannot take place without relying on the schematic working system.

The Semantic Working System

The semantic working system is what turns words into meaning. It isn't isolated incidents of identifying the main idea, sequencing, or cause and effect, for example, but rather the combination of all those and many other strategic activities that aid in formulating a whole. Your semantic working system is the system that enables you to remember what a story, movie, or event is about. Ask a friend or a colleague to tell you about his or her favorite book, show, or movie. More than likely, the person will share his or her feelings about it and give you the gist of the storyline without going into all the details. However, you might also get a detailed account, depending on the emotions stirred. That is the semantic working system functioning effectively.

The Pragmatic Working System

The pragmatic working system is the ability to understand the author's intent. It is the ability to pick up a computer magazine or an encyclopedia with the understanding that the authors of these documents wrote them with the purpose of informing the reader. That is not to say that Tolstoy, Dumas, or Twain didn't write with the purpose of informing us. We can be informed at a technological level and, at the same time, a humanistic level. Think about everything you've read today. Most of what people read on a daily basis is for information. The Internet, emails, the newspaper, magazines, and reports are written to inform us, and we read them to be informed even though the quality of the information can vary greatly. On the other hand, cartoon strips, romance novels, and horror thrillers are written to entertain and arouse emotions. A healthy diet of both is always recommended so that we feed our intellects and our hearts. Your pragmatic working system allows you to determine not only the author's purpose but also your purpose for reading a particular type of text. Depending on the reader, informational texts can also be read for entertainment, or as Louise Rosenblatt (1994) called it, for "efferent" or "aesthetic" reasons.

The Lexical Working System

The lexical working system is the knowledge of words. It includes the ability to use prefixes and suffixes, and to understand word origins and words from foreign languages. For example, we all understand that the prefix *anti* means against and the suffix *ism* means a belief. With that working knowledge, we're able to define such enigmatic words as *antidisestablishmentarianism*. Our lexical working system instantly kicks in to break the word apart and reassemble it in nano-seconds in order to understand it (*anti-dis-establish-ment-arian-ism*) beginning with the base word *establish.* It is your lexical working system that enables you to break a word apart and make sense of it.

Now think of the word *buffet* or *matinee* or *Collette.* What's the country of origin of those words? Most of us will recognize them as having a French origin. That's our lexical working system working for us. Notice, too, that it was our lexical working system coupled with our graphophonic working system that had us reading the "et" in *buffet* and the "ee" in *matinee* as a long /a/ vowel sound. *One working system functioning alone will not be enough to construct correct pronunciation and ultimately meaning*. We're constantly assembling and disassembling working systems to construct meaning. Essentially, the lexical working system can be defined as the sum of your knowledge of receptive (listening, viewing, reading) and expressive (speaking, writing) language. As we progress in our explanations, we want to revisit the concept that all systems are assembled and disassembled as we read a variety of texts for information or entertainment.

The Syntactic Working System

The syntactic working system is the understanding of the structure of language. It is knowing that language is rule governed and phrased in a certain predictable pattern in order to communicate and understand ourselves as well as each other. Your understanding of noun-verb agreement or that *an* precedes words that begin with vowel sounds and *a* precedes words that begin with a consonant is an example of your syntactic working system. Because of its relationship to oral language development, the syntactic working system develops early in young students (Clay, 2001).

We have briefly elaborated on six working systems that readers assemble and disassemble to construct meaning from print. The question now becomes: What do we do with all that information when we read? It's what we do with all those working systems that we call reading as a process. For all intents and purposes, and this is definitely an oversimplified explanation, the recursive process we're referring to starts with predicting and anticipating—a feedforward mechanism (Clay, 1998; Johnston, 1997)—followed by executing an action (in this case, reading), searching further at difficulty, and attempting to self-correct by rereading at different levels (word level, phrase level, sentence level, etc.) when something isn't quite right. Utilizing this process with a variety of strategic activities assists us in processing print to sustain the reading and to process print to expand the meaning or our understanding.

Figure 4.1 provides a graphic representation of this model. We've chosen a mobius to illustrate this process to highlight the in-and-out, back-and-forth recursive nature of reading as we engage in strategic activities to sustain the reading and expand meaning (Fountas & Pinnell, 2006). As Figure 4.1 illustrates, the assembling of working systems to sustain the reading propels the reader to assemble working systems that in turn expand meaning in a recursive pattern. Simultaneously, assembling working systems to expand meaning aids readers in assembling them to sustain their reading. It is complex. Figure 4.2 on page 45 lists a variety strategic activities that proficient readers use to sustain their reading and expand meaning from print. The list is meant to be illustrative and is

FIGURE 4.1

Literacy as a Process: A Framework for Guiding K–12 Learners

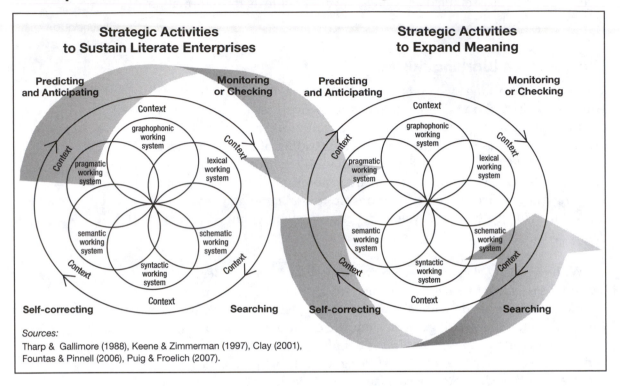

Sources:
Tharp & Gallimore (1988), Keene & Zimmerman (1997), Clay (2001),
Fountas & Pinnell (2006), Puig & Froelich (2007).

certainly not exhaustive. Many other strategic activities exist that many of us employ to construct meaning from print.

This type of theoretical conversation has the potential to be quite heady and esoteric, but it is a conversation that needs to take place over time if a literacy coach and a literacy leadership team want to make inroads in improving literacy instruction. Only through having these conversations can colleagues begin to develop a common language to enable all involved to defend the instructional practices used in classrooms. Agreeing or disagreeing is not the point. Talking is!

So, we have discussed the concept of reading as a process and the theoretical working systems that readers assemble and disassemble to sustain their reading and to expand meaning from print. With this understanding under our belt, we now need to consider what this process looks like over time and what are some developmental stages that learners go through to accomplish such a feat. Understanding the developmental stages of reading will impact the instructional practices that a literacy coach and

FIGURE 4.2

Strategic Activities to Sustain and Expand Literate Enterprises

Early Strategic Behaviors to Sustain Literate Enterprises	Strategic Activities to Sustain Literate Enterprises	Strategic Activities to Expand Meaning
One-to-one matching	Decoding	Making personal connections
Cross-checking	Segmenting words	Making intertectual connections
Locating known and unknown words	Blending words	Making global connections
Directionality (left to right, left page before right page, etc.)	Checking (monitoring)	Inferring
	Predicting	Summarizing
	Anticipating	Synthesizing
	Fluency	Analyzing
	Integrating	Critiquing
	Flexibility	Questioning
	Phrasing	Clarifying
	Word recognition	Visualizing
	Rereading	Evaluating
	Self-correcting	
	Searching further	

Note: Proficient readers use strategic activities to sustain learning and expand meaning fluidly before, during, and after literature enterprises. This list is illustrative, not exhaustive.

a literacy leadership team will eventually decide to implement based on documented data that focus on students' strengths and needs.

Developmental Stages of Reading

Students progress through developmental stages as they become more proficient readers (Chall, 1983). These developmental stages are not determined by grade level but by a student's experiences, understandings, attitudes, and expectations that the student has for reading and writing. Learning is continuous; the goal is to see where students are, notice their strengths, and then teach for strategic activity to promote forward shifts in literacy development (Pinnell & Fountas, 1998). Although these categories are roughly age related, it is obvious that there is a great deal of overlap with a lot of recursive activity. At the same time, the majority of students should be proficient readers by age 9.

Students who do not appear to be making satisfactory progress must have immediate intensive intervention with a strong diagnostic component and continuous assessment, preferably at an early age. The intervention must help students achieve accelerated progress in learning the critical skills and strategic activities of literacy. It must be well timed and consistent.

Developing Readers

Young learners are acquiring basic book-handling skills and are just learning that illustrations and books tell a story. Concurrently, the necessary phonological awareness skills are developing. These include the concept of spoken language; word rhyme recognition and production; syllable blending, segmentation, and deletion; and phoneme isolation, blending, segmentation, and deletion. Developing readers may also know letters, sounds, and high-frequency words. They use pictures and rely on their knowledge of oral language. With developing readers, teachers use a variety of delivery models and texts to support whole groups, small groups, and individuals in reading. The focus is on intentional instruction. Beginning books for this level should have natural language, a clear matching of pictures to text, repetitive text, and predictability. Decodable books are used, with the clear understanding that the ability to decode is relative to the learner, the content, and the context. At this stage students often memorize the text as part of the developmental process. This occurs for most students between the ages of 5 and 7.

This stage of development is generally known as *emergent*. In 2001, Dr. Marie M. Clay, known for coining the phrase *emergent readers*, wrote that due to so many misunderstandings and interpretations of the phrase, she has abandoned the term. *Developing readers* defines this stage more accurately, since the word *developing* implies growing or evolving rather than emergent, which implies arising or occurring unexpectedly. Consequently, we have adopted the term *developing reader*.

Early Readers

At this stage of development, conventional reading is beginning to occur. These young students are developing strategic activities for reading and self-correction. Students at this point of development demonstrate integrating a variety of sources of information, search further at difficulty, reread for different reasons, and begin to read silently with occasional lapses into reading aloud. Sources of information for these readers are their background experiences, vocabulary, knowledge of sounds and letters, print itself, and illustrations. As readers become more sophisticated, other sources of information develop. To better understand the concept of sources of information, think of all the information you rely on when you're reading to construct meaning or a defensible interpretation.

In working with students at this stage, the teacher's role is to deliver intentional instruction in decoding (graphophonic system), vocabulary development (lexical system) and comprehension (assembling system). Once the teacher has introduced the text, these students can read appropriately selected materials. This stage occurs for most students between the ages of 6 and 8.

Transitional Readers

Learners soon gain enough control of reading so that self-correction is automatic. They have a large core of known words that are recognized automatically and have flexible ways of seeking solutions to construct meaning. Reading is phrased and fluent at appropriate levels, and strategic activities in reading are used effectively, flexibly, and efficiently. Students use the illustrations to gain additional meaning and interpret the meaning in an informational text. They understand how to read differently in a variety of genres by purposefully assembling a pragmatic working system with other working systems to understand an author's intent. Silent reading gradually becomes a natural form of behavior. This stage occurs for most students between the ages of 7 and 9.

Self-Extending Readers

In the next stage, learners have systems in place for learning more about processing information as they read so that they build skills simply by encountering different genres with a variety of new vocabulary. They are in a continuous process of building background knowledge (schematic system) and realize that they need to bring their knowledge to their reading. Students make personal, intertextual, and global connections more consistently and become absorbed in books. They sustain reading texts with many pages that may require many days or weeks to read. The children use many sources of information flexibly, such as meaning (semantic system), structure of the language (syntactic system), phonics (graphophonic system), word knowledge (lexical system), author's intent or purpose (pragmatic system), and prior knowledge (schematic system), including the illustrations to interpret and use information from both non-narrative and narrative texts. They read silently and fluently most of the time. This stage occurs for most students between the ages of 8 and 10.

Advanced Readers

At this stage of literacy acquisition, learners consistently go beyond the text being read to form their own interpretations and apply understandings in other areas. They acquire new vocabulary through reading and use reading as a tool for learning in content areas. They actively work to connect texts for deeper understanding and finer interpretation. The readers know how to direct their attention depending on the kind of text being read. For example, they may read a text primarily to gain information or for pleasure. Their attention is focused in specific ways and their goal is to increase their knowledge. They sustain interest and understanding over long texts and read silently over extended periods of time. They begin to notice writing styles and develop favorite topics and authors that form the basis of life-long reading preferences. This stage occurs for most students at about the age of 10 or older.

Although we have listed the stages of development in a very linear fashion, learners do not necessarily learn in a linear fashion, leading us to state that there may be cases where some students may skip (or temporarily skip) a stage and move forward or backward depending on the text and context. In the next section of this chapter, we're going to show how to theoretically bridge the use of the same working systems when we write.

At this point, a reminder may be needed. The reason for reviewing and discussing reading and writing at such a theoretical level is that unless a literacy coach and a literacy leadership team have a clear understanding of how readers process print and develop in a literate environment, data will invariably be misinterpreted, consequently misguiding instructional practices that have the potential to negatively influence learning (Clay, 2001; Gillion, 2004). Remember that one of the main purposes for establishing leadership teams is so the literacy programs at school can evolve and develop appropriately to support student learning. Additionally, if a literacy coach or a literacy leadership team is to defend its decisions to improve instruction, this theoretical understanding has to be in place. Without it, the literacy coach and the literacy leadership team will be hard pressed to sell their decisions not only to the rest of the faculty but also to district administrators and the community.

In middle school and high school, this understanding becomes even more critical because the literacy leadership team has to promote their decisions to colleagues in a variety of content areas. When speaking with colleagues from different content areas, keep in mind that the only common thread of conversations to take place is "learning" and "how students learn." Effective and efficient middle school and high school literacy leadership teams rarely address reading and writing as a process with content area colleagues. Rather, middle and high school literacy leadership teams speak of learning as a process. If your conversations adhere to learning and how students learn, you are more likely to get your content area colleagues engaged and excited about the changes the literacy leadership team recommends to improve learning and instruction across the board. Moreover, experienced educators in elementary, middle, and high schools have gotten away from the learning-to-read reading-to-learn mentality because they have realized that in many cases this double standards theory of literacy learning has created a chasm in instruction across grade levels. *Effective and efficient literacy leadership teams work from the understanding that readers are always learning to read and reading to learn concurrently and not consecutively.* The theoretical dichotomy of the dual-level theory of literacy acquisition is considered passé by many experts in the field.

Writing as a Process

The best example we can provide to help us focus on writing is to think of the processes that you go through when writing anything. *All writing, even responding to reading, involves a process where we mentally or physically rehearse and compose, execute an action by constructing print or writing, revise, edit, and maybe publish.* We need to remember that a lot of one's writing is never taken to a final publishing level, but remains in draft form.

Think of a time you made the decision to write or were asked (usually required, particularly in school) to write. Most of us start by thinking about what we're going to write and who our audience will be. If our schematic working system is weak on a particular subject, we search or research further on this to build our background knowledge and expand our understanding. Note that the act of mental rehearsal requires us to assemble and dissemble various working systems to organize our thinking before actually constructing (writing) the text. Some writers organize their thinking by using graphic organizers, while others organize their thinking during the act of writing itself. Regardless of how a writer organizes her or his thinking, once sufficient background knowledge and a sense of audience develop, the writer constructs the text. Even while constructing the text, rehearsal or composing is taking place. The evidence for this is shown in the many times that virtually all writers revise while engaged in the act of writing. Searching or researching further, as we have stated, occurs when a writer re-visions—that is, he or she develops images of the text, or revises the text that is written. Writers search further for a variety of reasons. Again, think of a writing enterprise that you've attempted to execute. When something wasn't quite right, you revised the text. It could be that an idea wasn't expressed clearly. In some cases, it could be that a misspelling or unconventional grammar caught your eye so you felt the need to revise.

As writers, we often rely on resources to help us revise. If it's at the conceptual level, we may research more on the subject or talk with colleagues. If it's at the print level, we may consult a dictionary, a spell-checker, or a thesaurus. Nonetheless, we all search further once we engage in the act of writing.

After searching further, and using the necessary resources to do so, we do the actual adjustment of re-visioning or editing. Think of searching further as evidenced by erasing (on paper) or deleting (on the computer), and adjusting comes to fruition when we rewrite or retype. Every time we email a friend or colleague and we delete and retype certain words or phrases, for whatever reason, we are engaging in searching and adjusting the text we're constructing.

We want to point out that in the act of writing, we are still basically processing the invisible text in our heads in order to make it visible, in order to communicate with others if that's our intent. The audience plays a pivotal role in writing. Whether we're writing to entertain or inform others or simply to assist us in remembering, the pragmatic working system (our sense of purpose) is assembled and disassembled with the other aforementioned working systems to assist us in constructing meaningful text for a specific reason.

As in understanding reading as a process, understanding writing as a process is necessary to aid literacy coaches and literacy leadership teams in making informed decisions that promote forward shifts in instruction for all students. All content or subject areas in elementary, middle, and high school require students to write at some level. We therefore encourage you to go beyond this book to investigate the impact of writing on learning across grade levels and content areas to support students seamlessly as they progress through the grades. We also want to reiterate to literacy coaches and literacy leadership teams that in any act of writing—regardless of whether it is responding to reading, generating an informative piece, or an entertaining narrative—we all go through a process to turn the invisible text in our heads into visible text that can be read. Next, we'll investigate the reciprocal nature of reading and writing as a support or scaffold for student learning.

Reciprocity of Literate Activities

We've reviewed reading and writing as a process, highlighting the commonalities between the two processes. Although not identical, they are certainly mutually supportive of each other. On the one hand, we read and reread to generate ideas in writing and to improve our writing. On the other hand, we write to remember what we have read and to clarify our thinking about what we have read. Effective and efficient classroom teachers and literacy coaches know how to incorporate various instructional practices that immerse students in an information-intensive environment and to engage them in literate enterprises that rely on the reciprocity of reading and writing.

Regretfully, we have witnessed many classroom programs, school-level initiatives, and district-level initiatives that do not take advantage of the reciprocal nature of reading and writing, potentially increasing the likelihood of forcing students into becoming learning disabled by well-intentioned initiatives. *Programs,* as we define it, are not just a series of published materials by a particular publishing company, but rather a series or framework of instructional practices used to support and promote learning. Effective programs, whether as we have defined it or a published series of materials, provide teachers, literacy coaches, and literacy leadership teams a variety of opportunities to observe, assess, and evaluate how well students are learning. It has been our experience that it is only through a well-organized series of literacy experiences that we can truly make a judgment call on how students are learning. Well-organized programs allow us to collect static and dynamic assessments. *Informed literacy coaches and literacy leadership teams take advantage of the reciprocal nature of reading and writing to promote literate enterprises across content areas in all grade levels.*

While investigating an adaptive challenge for the school, we highly recommend that the literacy coach and the literacy leadership team keep the reciprocal nature of reading and writing at the forefront of the investigation. Doing so will economize on teachers' time and intentionally amplify instruction for the students to promote accelerated learning, particularly for low-progress students who need to catch up to their peers in class. Think of the reciprocity of reading and writing as getting two for one. In today's activity-packed school schedules, a single instructional practice can be used to scaffold learning in a content area by utilizing and highlighting the benefit of reading to writing and writing to reading when providing a focus-lesson to students.

Teaching for Strategic Activity to Sustain Literate Enterprises and Expand Meaning

Up to this point in the chapter we have addressed stages of development, reading, writing, the reciprocal benefit of one to the other, and the importance of literacy coaches and literacy leadership teams understanding this information. All this information would certainly count for nothing if we didn't address the impact and relationship it has to learning and instruction—specifically, teaching for strategic activity. When we talk about teaching for strategic activity, we are referring to intentional teaching that focuses on teaching students to become critical, independent, and flexible learners. In other words, we are focusing our teaching on assisting students to be self-directed, self-regulating, and self-extending (Clay, 2001). Thus, the big question always arises: How do we know if we are teaching *for* strategic activity?

Before we go on, note that we used the preposition *for* rather than saying "teaching strategic activities" because we define strategic activities as a mental call to action. Since strategic activities in literate enterprises are generally "in the head," we cannot see them and we cannot teach them directly, but we can certainly teach "for" them to take place by our language and the instructional practices we employ.

Literacy coaches and literacy leadership teams (since they are made up primarily of classroom teachers) witness teaching for strategic activity when teachers teach at the students' instructional level or zone of proximal development (Vygotsky, 1978). At their instructional levels, students are provided the opportunity to seek solutions within a balance of supports and challenges. In an extremely simplistic explanation, teaching for strategic activity follows an I-do—you-look, I-do—you-help, You-do—I-help, You-do—I-look format. The operative word is *do.* In the field of education this is known as a *gradual release model of executive control.*

The teacher who is teaching for strategic activity will plan lessons that account for the following:

1. Materials need to be at the students' instructional level (generally material that they can read with 90 to 94 percent accuracy).

2. Generative responses are provided rather than corrective feedback.

3. Teaching prompts promote independent problem solving.

4. Reciprocity between reading and writing enterprises are highlighted.

5. If materials are above the students' instructional level, a variety of instructional practices are employed to scaffold instruction (Bruner, 1990).

6. Static and dynamic assessments are used to guide instruction.

7. Assessment is ongoing to monitor change over time.

Although these are some simple guidelines to gauge whether instruction is aimed at teaching for strategic activity, simply adhering to the guidelines does not guarantee that teaching for strategic activity is taking place. Yet, conscientiously keeping these guidelines on the forefront of thinking when planning lessons will increase the likelihood that teaching for strategic activity will be promoted. A serious point of consideration for literacy coaches, as they guide and support literacy leadership teams, is that the seven guidelines apply to teachers at all grade levels and all content areas. A productive exercise for the team is to list the seven guidelines and provide an explanation of how each applies to each content area (language arts, mathematics, science, social studies, art, and music). Since this is critical information for literacy coaches and literacy leadership teams, in the next few paragraphs we'll elaborate on each of the guidelines

When teaching for strategic activities, teachers should use materials that are at the students' instructional level. When materials are too difficult, strategic activities begin to disintegrate, with readers generally relying solely on the graphophonic working system to simply decode words at the letter level, and we do not want students to walk away thinking that reading is just an act of decoding words on a page. Although decoding words can be a powerful strategic activity when assembled with other working systems, by itself it does not get the reader/learner closer to constructing meaning or generating a defensible interpretation (our definition of comprehension). Without constructing meaning, any act of learning is diminished if nonexistent. For example, if someone asks you to read a medical text or a highly technical computer journal of which you do not have the background knowledge or vocabulary, you are likely to simply decode words and not comprehend. If there is a lack of background knowledge and critical content vocabulary, you will not be able to construct meaning from the text or journal. The exact situation occurs to students in schools when they are asked to read materials that are beyond their cognitive or maturity level. Effective teaching for strategic activity relies heavily on providing students with materials at levels they can comprehend with either assistance or independently.

When teaching for strategic activity, teachers provide generative responses rather than corrective feedback (which tends to remove the responsibility of learning from the student). *Strategic activity* is synonymous with *active solution seeking*. Over time, we have chosen to use the phrase *solution seeking* rather than *problem solving* because it reflects a more positive desirable behavior. Hence, active solution seeking cannot occur when teachers remove the responsibility of learning by correcting the student and providing the right answer. Alternatively, when providing a generative response, the responsibility for learning is left with the student, with the teacher prompting the student to utilize what he or she knows to get to the unknown.

Consequently, the teaching prompts used to promote independent solution-seeking behavior become a critical arsenal for teachers. Armed with knowledge of instructional practices and language, teachers have the power to make or break a learning moment. Prompted by the work of Tharp and Gallimore (1988), one question that we have learned to ask ourselves over time when prompting students for strategic activity is: Am I assisting or assessing students' performance? The types of prompts or questions we ask students always have the potential to be interpreted as helping or testing. Although at times we do want to ask questions that assess performance, if our goal is to teach for strategic activity we need to measure our words carefully to ensure that our prompts are assisting performance by engaging students in active solution-seeking behavior (Johnston, 2004).

Most schooling deals with learning from print. Teaching for reciprocity between reading and writing enterprises economizes students' cognitive load by always highlighting how one supports the other. The reciprocity between reading and writing buttresses strategic activities across content areas as students construct meaning. For teachers, this means that our overt conversations during learning moments need to intentionally focus on how one activity supports another and the benefit to the student.

Realistically, we know that not all materials that students are exposed to can be at their instructional level. When that is the case and materials are above the students' instructional level, a variety of instructional practices are employed to scaffold instruction (Bruner, 1990). By *scaffolding instruction*, we're referring to the previously mentioned model of learning and instruction that focuses on the I-do—you-look, I-do—you-help, You-do—I-help, You-do—I-look format. This gradual release model of executive control creates a safe environment for students to ensure engagement and exposure to new vocabulary over time that will serve students well when independently seeking solutions.

All of us have heard over and over the mantra that assessment should guide instruction. Yet seldom do we hear what type of assessment we should rely on to ensure that we employ powerful instructional practices that are a good match for students. Teachers who teach for strategic activity rely on static and dynamic assessments (Dixon-Krauss, 1996). *Static assessments* are summative assessments that tell you, in general terms, what your students are learning in relation to other students or what your students are learning in a specific content area. This is vital information in order for teachers to gauge their overall teaching and content. Static assessments are state tests, chapter tests, and the like. *Dynamic assessments* refer to formative assessments that hone in on your students' strengths and needs. Static assessments potentially reveal *what* students have learned; dynamic assessments potentially reveal *how* students learn. One focuses on outcomes and the other focuses on process. Therefore, teaching for strategic activity means relying on static and dynamic assessment to make informed decisions that support student learning.

Conventional wisdom and experience teaches us that learning occurs and changes over time. Monitoring and documenting those changes is critical when teaching for strategic activity. A teacher's classroom is packed with split-second decision making throughout the day. Unfortunately, the human memory can hold only so much for so long before information is replaced with new information. Consequently, when our intention is to teach powerfully, our students' learning has to be monitored and documented in order for assessment to truly guide instruction. Thus, to teach for strategic activity means ongoing monitoring and documenting our students' strengths and needs.

As literacy leadership teams move forward beyond an initial adaptive challenge to design a plan for the school, all members need to remember that ultimately they want to support and nurture students in becoming strategic learners. The goal is not to make it easy. Rather, the goal is to make it easy to learn. Only by teaching students how to learn can we ensure that we are supporting students in becoming self-extending learners. The language we use and the instructional practices we employ certainly impacts whether we accomplish that goal.

Summary

Throughout this text we will consistently and continually keep repeating and referring to the two major concepts that form a strong foundation for any literacy coach and literacy leadership team. Those two concepts are that literacy coaches, literacy leadership teams, and schools have to develop a *common language* and they need to have a clear understanding of *literacy as a process* to sustain and expand success. Both in the literature and in our many years of experience in working with literacy coaches and literacy leadership teams, we have found that when a common language and a clear understanding of literacy as a process is not established in the beginning, the data are misinterpreted and instructional practices are misguided. This in turn has the potential to impact student learning negatively.

In this chapter we briefly discussed the developmental stages of reading and literacy as a process as a conceptual framework of working systems with a dual purpose of sustaining learning and expanding learning (Figure 4.1). We also discussed the reciprocal nature of reading and writing and the benefit to student learning by highlighting how literacy coaches, literacy leadership teams, and teachers can teach for strategic activity to support strategic learners.

The ideas and concepts presented are intended to promote critical thinking on the part of literacy coaches and literacy leadership teams before identifying an initial adaptive challenge based on student data. The ideas of understanding adult learning, conditions for learning, developing a common language, understanding literacy development, and understanding literacy as a process are paramount not only to the success of the literacy leadership team but also to sustaining and expanding that success. These are the concrete and steel of a powerful foundation to support the work of both the literacy coach and the literacy leadership team in sustaining and expanding success.

In the next chapter, we will begin reviewing and recommending logistical information to support literacy leadership teams across all grade levels. Starting off with setting some basic ground rules to identifying members at elementary and secondary schools, we will tie the work to creating a generative system that focuses on assessing strengths and needs, creating and executing a plan, reflecting on the successes and limitations of the plan, and reassessing to continue.

LIBRETTO

Betty really wanted to be a part of the literacy leadership team. She knew there was much to be learned and that she had been out of the loop as far as research was concerned for too long. She saw this as an opportunity to get her in-service points, and help her students at the same time. The problem was that her other team members in the social studies department thought she was nuts. They didn't see any reason to do the reading specialist's (or for that matter, the language arts teachers in the middle schools) job. Her team told her over and over that her job was to teach government and that she shouldn't worry about whether the students were reading successfully. They believed that there would always be a percentage of students who failed and that some students wouldn't be able to write an essay to save their lives. Betty was really tired of them beating her down with this argument and she really wanted to have the knowledge to be able to stand her ground. So far, though, she was losing the battle.

Reflections

1. As a member of the literacy leadership team, what would you advise Betty about joining the team?

2. How can joining the team benefit Betty?

3. What can Betty say to her colleagues that would not alienate them?

Exchange

In the "'X-ed' Change," Mary and Jackie were lacking in some basic knowledge that would help them make a more informed decision when it comes to adopting texts. What are some of the things that, as the literacy coach or a member of the team, you would tell them that could get their intellectual curiosity started? What would you have them read that would be beneficial? If the end result were that neither of them wanted to engage in change, what would you say to them, to the administration, and to the parents if you were given the opportunity?

Chapter 5

Getting Started

"X-ed" Change

Mary and Gene were assigned as the literacy coaches to the high school and Bruce was to coach at the elementary school. During their weekly meeting with the literacy coordinator, one part of the agenda was about how they would organize the teams for their respective schools.

Mary: In my school, I have already been told by the principal to choose the members. He told me that I should look at the schedule and choose people who don't have a club or after-school assignment. That pretty much guarantees that the coaches can't participate, nor the music teachers. So it looks like we will have the usual group of people: one teacher each from math, science, social studies, and English/language Arts, maybe a counselor, and one administrator, but not the principal—he said he was too busy this year but that he would try to sit in from time to time. We haven't even started yet, and I am already frustrated.

Gene: Well, it looks like this may have been a county mandate, because I have been told the exact same thing about the high school team. How can they expect that we can have a really strong team if everyone isn't represented? I wanted each discipline to be a part of the decision making. I guess I'm going to have to settle for what I can get.

Bruce: My school will have one representative from each of the grade levels plus music and art. I will also have an administrator but I don't know who yet. I wanted a fifth-grade student to be a part as well, but the principal shot that idea down. She said that the fifth-graders were too busy getting ready for sixth grade and she didn't think they should be called on to stay after school to attend the meetings. I really thought the county was behind us starting these literacy leadership teams. Now I'm wondering what I've gotten myself into.

Please read the chapter and after reading the libretto and reflections, decide what these three coaches should do so that they will have a better chance of having successful literacy leadership teams.

As in any new endeavor, getting started is always the hardest step. Starting a literacy leadership team is no different. We have found that beginning with a self-assessment provides the team with long-term goals and direction in establishing a literacy leadership team that will sustain and expand success in any school setting. Consequently, the very first meeting of the literacy leadership team or the first meeting of a group of colleagues interested in establishing a literacy leadership team needs to involve a self-assessment to gauge the plausibility of moving forward in establishing the team. Group members need to understand from the start the purposes and goals of literacy leadership teams at school sites. Figure 5.1 is a self-assessment survey any school—elementary, middle, or high school—can use to start investigating the collective and individual roles of members on a literacy leadership team. The survey is not meant to be a measuring stick, but rather a guidepost for a group to see where they need to go to ensure sustaining and expanding success at their schools. In other words, the group or team needs to take a critical and honest look at themselves if forward shifts are to occur.

After completing the Literacy Leadership Team Self-Assessment Survey (Figure 5.1), group or team members tally their collective responses to arrive at an overall picture of what it is going to take for the team to be successful in supporting forward shifts in learning and instruction at their school. With that information under their belt, the team now needs to make the decision whether to proceed as a literacy leadership team with strong guidance from a knowledgeable literacy coach.

Proceeding forward, the team's next step is to define and establish ground rules for functioning effectively and efficiently during the tight schedule of a school day. Throughout the process of establishing ground rules, developing a common language will be an ongoing process as more is learned while researching and tackling an adaptive challenge. With ground rules set, the group assembles a working system to support change that involves group members in creating a framework for the team to follow. By assembling a working system or framework, team routines and rituals will be put in place, allowing members not just to think outside the box, but to investigate and create their own boxes to think outside of.

FIGURE 5.1
Literacy Leadership Team Self-Assessment Survey

The Literacy Leadership Team Self-Assessment Survey is designed for schools interested in utilizing a literacy leadership team supported by a literacy coach. This survey is but one instrument that supports schools in taking inventory of what is in place to promote forward shifts in learning and instruction. Assessment, particularly self-assessment, is a critical first step in determining where to start. After completing the survey, the total number of "very accurate" and "accurate" responses will provide you with a general idea of the present potential to sustain and expand success at your school. It is a starting point, not a determining point.

Schools are complex systems for learning and instruction, influenced by politics, economics, languages, and cultures. No single instrument of assessment can ever truly provide the necessary information to promote transformations in learning and instruction. This survey is meant to be cross-checked or triangulated with participant and nonparticipant observations to arrive at an accurate picture of existing strengths and needs.

Directions: Mark the statement that best describes your school. After completing the survey, total the number of "very accurate" and "accurate" responses.

1. The school Literacy Leadership Team consists of representatives from a variety of grade levels and/or content areas.
   ❏ very accurate   ❏ accurate   ❏ somewhat accurate   ❏ inaccurate   ❏ very inaccurate

2. There is a district Literacy Leadership Team to collaborate with the school Literacy Leadership Team.
   ❏ very accurate   ❏ accurate   ❏ somewhat accurate   ❏ inaccurate   ❏ very inaccurate

3. The Literacy Coach is the "lead learner" responsible for the professional learning of the school faculty and Literacy Leadership Team.
   ❏ very accurate   ❏ accurate   ❏ somewhat accurate   ❏ inaccurate   ❏ very inaccurate

4. The school Literacy Leadership Team investigates multiple sources of data (static and dynamic) to determine students' strengths and needs.
   ❏ very accurate   ❏ accurate   ❏ somewhat accurate   ❏ inaccurate   ❏ very inaccurate

5. The school Literacy Leadership Team investigates multiple sources of data (static and dynamic) to determine faculty and staff's strengths and needs.
   ❏ very accurate   ❏ accurate   ❏ somewhat accurate   ❏ inaccurate   ❏ very inaccurate

6. The school Literacy Leadership Team determines a specific adaptive challenge for the school or each grade level or content area based on data (static and dynamic).
   ❏ very accurate   ❏ accurate   ❏ somewhat accurate   ❏ inaccurate   ❏ very inaccurate

7. An action plan has been developed based on analyzed data (static and dynamic) by the Literacy Leadership Team.
   ❏ very accurate   ❏ accurate   ❏ somewhat accurate   ❏ inaccurate   ❏ very inaccurate

8. The school principal and the literacy coach attend all Literacy Leadership Team meetings.
   ❏ very accurate   ❏ accurate   ❏ somewhat accurate   ❏ inaccurate   ❏ very inaccurate

9. The school Literacy Leadership Team meets monthly for at least one hour.
   ❏ very accurate   ❏ accurate   ❏ somewhat accurate   ❏ inaccurate   ❏ very inaccurate

10. The school's action plan includes a five-stage implementation framework to ensure sustainability and expansion.
    ❏ very accurate   ❏ accurate   ❏ somewhat accurate   ❏ inaccurate   ❏ very inaccurate

11. The school has a designated block of time for reading/language arts.
    ❏ very accurate   ❏ accurate   ❏ somewhat accurate   ❏ inaccurate   ❏ very inaccurate

12. The school provides an intervention outside of the regular literacy block of time or language arts period for low-progress students.
    ❏ very accurate   ❏ accurate   ❏ somewhat accurate   ❏ inaccurate   ❏ very inaccurate

10–12	very accurate or accurate statements:	Strong potential for sustaining and expanding success
8–9	very accurate or accurate statements:	Above-average potential for sustaining and expanding success
6–7	very accurate or accurate statements:	Developing potential for expanding and sustaining success
4–5	very accurate or accurate statements:	Below-average potential for expanding and sustaining success
2–3	very accurate or accurate statements:	Weak potential for sustaining and expanding success

Note: The Literacy Leadership Team Self-Assessment Survey is meant to prompt and guide discussion. It was not designed or intended to serve as an evaluative instrument.

In addition, team member identification will be critical to provide the literacy leadership team with multiple perspectives that will strengthen the team's decision to impact learning and instruction in a variety of grade levels and content area classrooms. Consequently, although in function, a literacy leadership team at the elementary and the secondary level may be similar, the makeup of the team is different.

Defining the Ground Rules

As in all of aspects of communication, to establish a common language it is important for all team members to understand what we mean when we talk about "ground rules." We must all have the same appreciation for the rules and how they apply to us individually and as a member of the group. These rules can cover the behavior of the group members, the role of each member, and perhaps even the rules about how discussions take place. Maiese (2004) refers to these rules as *protocols*. These would be the rules that the group generates during their first meeting that sets the tone for future meetings. These protocols can include:

- Project organization
- Decision making
- Communication with others
- Using data and technical information
- Setting procedural rules

Project organization refers to how each member is assigned the work to be accomplished. The team leader usually starts the first meeting with an outline of what the team will be expected to accomplish over the course of the year. Sometimes roles are assigned, but many times group members are asked to volunteer for assignments. Figure 5.2 shows two models of how some teams might operate. Look over these two models and make any adjustments you want to meet your team's needs. The first model is one that uses six team members plus the literacy coach as the team leader. The second one assumes that the literacy coach would start as the team leader but that after the initial meeting, the team leadership would rotate to other members. If you have more group members than seven total, you might want to have a model that allows group members to rotate in and out of positions as the year progresses.

The members serve as moderator, scribe, data collector, disseminator, hostess/host, and group librarian. The moderator is responsible for making sure that the team stays on task and that everyone is on the "same page" during the meetings. When a conflict arises, the moderator helps dissipate the issue with as little disruption to the meeting as possible. The scribe takes the minutes of the meeting and ensures that all team members get a full accounting of what occurred during the meeting. This information is also provided in full to the disseminator, who then has the responsibility of passing this along to other significant personnel (i.e., administrators not involved with the team). The data collector is responsible for gathering any evidence that the group compiles or data that they will need to complete their assignments. The hostess/host is responsible for securing the appropriate room and providing any refreshments for that meeting. (This position should rotate regularly.) The role of the group librarian is to make sure that any reading material (e.g., articles, books) are available to each team member. There may be other tasks that your team will take on and these roles can be assigned as needed.

Decision making refers to who will make the decisions regarding what issues will be examined, how the data will be collected, and how it will

FIGURE 5.2
Hierarchy of Team Structure

Model One: Year-Long Team Plan	
Team Leader (The Literacy Coach)	
Team Member 1 (moderator)	Team Member 4 (disseminator)
Team Member 2 (scribe)	Team Member 5 (hostess/host)
Team Member 3 (data collector)	Team Member 6 (group librarian)
Model Two: Per Meeting Plan	
Meeting 1: Literacy Coach leads group	
Team Member 1 (moderator)	Team Member 4 (disseminator)
Team Member 2 (scribe)	Team Member 5 (hostess/host)
Team Member 3 (data collector)	Team Member 6 (group librarian)
Meeting 2: Team Member 1 (Group Leader)	
Team Member 2 (moderator)	Team Member 5 (disseminator)
Team Member 3 (scribe)	Team Member 6 (hostess/host)
Team Member 4 (date collector)	Team Member 7 (Literacy Coach) (group librarian)

be disseminated to others. How we *communicate with others* is part of this as well. The group will determine whether weekly, biweekly, or monthly reporting to the administration or the faculty as a whole will be the format. *Using the data and technical information* is crucial to the success of the team.

With the heavy use of computers, it is important to remember that all email correspondence should be copied to all team members every time there is information to be relayed. If this isn't done, you run the risk of creating a "political" situation—one where some team members do not feel as valued as others. If it has to do with the literacy leadership team, all members should be included in correspondence. The group should determine whether they will use email to discuss group discussions, whether they will establish a group discussion forum on the computer, and whether appropriate outside personnel will have access to their findings during the report building process.

Another key feature of understanding the terms of ground rules is knowing what is meant by *setting procedural rules.* These can be protocols such as those that determine whether the team allows "observers," those people who are not part of the regular team, for example. All protocols need to be in place before the team can start to function as a single unit. Having clear definitions of what these things mean will help setting the ground rules a lot easier.

Setting the Ground Rules

Envision a school community that has a literacy leadership team in place. See this team as one that is cohesive and well grounded. This team would have a sense of inquisitiveness. They would see change as growth, not as something regressive. They would challenge each other to think deeply, to read broadly, and to write coherently about literacy issues so that their school is one of continuous improvement.

The leadership team should be able to establish ground rules—rules that address such issues as "What are the protocols for answering questions?" For example, do we raise our hands, or just speak when there is an opportunity? There should be guidelines for the participants to generate such rules within the team. Some of these might include the following:

- Always be respectful of others when they are speaking.

- When talking, try to use your own experiences.

- Always be punctual and attend the assigned meetings.

- Try to value others' experiences.

- Try to explore common as well as divergent themes.

- Be appreciative of other responses by giving appropriate feedback.

- Be open and honest.

- Find things you have in common.

- Check your ego at the door.

Finding ways to make sure that everyone is comfortable in the group doesn't just include making sure the members "know" each other. It must also include a welcoming environment—a place that isn't too hot or too cold, a place that has appropriate space for everyone, and a place that has enough space for writing and taking notes. It's also a good idea to provide food—we all love to discuss over a good meal, so whenever possible try to have your meetings with food. You can ask different members to contribute each meeting ("Tips for Working Successfully in a Group," 2001).

Other types of rules that can help the team become more effective could include the following:

- We will actively attend and participate in regularly scheduled meetings.
- We will complete all assigned readings and come prepared to discuss.
- We will help create and evaluate data collected by team members.
- We will complete required assignments on time.
- We will cooperate with other team members.

There are several reasons for establishing the ground rules before the team tries to collect data and affect change in the schools. Some of these are that team rule building encourages collaboration, makes each member a stakeholder in the development of the rules, and encourages members to feel safe to participate. Other considerations that this might provide are setting the tone for interaction and establishing respect, openness, and sensitivity to other team members (www.gsi.berkeley.edu). Although there are other guidelines that your team might generate as well, the following are critical questions that group members should consider:

- Who are effective team members?
- How are effective team members chosen?
- What do we, as individuals, think the role of the team is?
- What are our goals as a team?
- How will we accomplish these goals?
- What are the critical aspects of our roles as team members?
- What guidelines will we establish for meetings?
- How will we establish critical rules?
- How will we determine what data to collect?
- How will we collect data?
- How will we report our findings to others (faculty and administrators)?

According to data reported from www.ecademy.com, only one-third of those attending meetings actually say anything. Other important data report that men talk in groups more often than women and that they are more likely to interrupt others when speaking. Also worth mentioning is that most men defined a "good conversation" as one in which *they* were in control, whereas women defined it as one in which *everyone* took turns speaking. This is vitally important information to the literacy leadership team members if they are going to have a successful experience.

The following section examines three methods that have been used to help establish the group dynamics. These are the acronym method, the small-group method, and the Brookfield and Preskill method.

Acronym Method

There are several methods for setting team goals and purposes. In the first of these, the *acronym method,* the literacy coach, as team leader, writes a word on a board or a piece of poster paper. She or he asks the team members to think about words that go with each of the letters of the word. For example, say you used the acronym *TEAM* to set your mission: TEAM could stand for "Talking, Evaluating, Accepting, Mentoring." This would give the team members a quick way to think about the rules for talking, evaluating performance, accepting each others' work product, and mentoring each other. It is important to remember that the expectations of both the leader and the members should be respected and incorporated if the team is to be successful.

Small-Group Method

Another established method is the *small-group method* developed by Heather McCarty at the University of California, Berkeley. The team leader divides the team members into small groups of three or four and gives each member an index card. He or she then asks each person to write down two rules that the individual thinks are really important. The team leader should give each group about five or ten minutes to complete this task. The group then discusses each of these and tries to reach consensus on the five or six that they feel are the most important. The group should revisit these rules periodically to see if they are working and what should be done if they aren't.

Brookfield and Preskill's Method

The last method is the *Brooksfield and Preskill's method* (1999). This method asks the group members to think about positive and negative aspects of group discussion. The team members need to generate three issues that would help create change so that there is always (as much as possible) positive discussion. They would then draft a list, record the new rules, and, from time to time, revisit them so that they can accurately evaluate how the rules are working. This would be a great time to discuss, for example, what to do when one person seems to be dominating a discussion. The team leader should not be afraid to include her or his experiences and might even include ones that the leader viewed as leading to unsuccessful group mentoring.

Assembling a Working System to Support Change

Each coach knows the importance of having a strong working system and how to assemble this system so that effective, long-term change can be made (Puig & Froelich, 2007). Just as there are working systems of reading, there is a working system that must be in place for literacy leadership teams to be effective. Each member of the team must be well versed in the components that comprise this system. These are:

- Common goals
- Understanding literacy
- Co-Learning
- Professional growth

Common Goals

Each member of the team should have a desire to help promote successful and sustained change. Team members should establish goals before they attempt to tackle the literacy issues that they are attempting to change. They must understand that the literacy development of all students is at the heart of these goals.

Understanding Literacy

Each member of the team should know the working systems for literacy (identified in Chapter 4) and understand that each one is important so that comprehending can take place. Team members should also know that these working systems include such things as oral language development, listening skills, and writing. Finally, team members should be cognizant of how these systems are assembled by students in the classroom (Puig & Froelich, 2007). All team members need to be able to evaluate and assess these working systems so that they know when the systems are and are not working appropriately.

Co-Learning

Literacy leadership team members should see themselves as co-learners. That is, they must be able to decide as a group that the mission and goals they are trying to achieve are best delivered when the members arrive at the end together. The coach helps the team members see him or her as a partner in learning, not as someone who dictates the parameters for the team. When one team member finds something interesting in the literature and wants to share it with the others, it should be seen as an attempt to disseminate information, not trying to point out how "well read" the team member is. She or he should be thought of as someone who is trying to further the goals of the entire team.

Professional Growth

People involved in working with the literacy leadership team must see this as a prime opportunity to continue their personal and professional growth. Stigler and Hiebert (1999) believe that "teachers need opportunities for sustained professional learning" and that schools need to be places where not only students but also teachers can learn. Hord (1997) believes that schools should be "communities of continuous inquiry and improvement." Certainly, literacy leadership teams provide a wonderful opportunity for continual growth and inquiry.

Identifying Members

Who are the team members? Should they be chosen by the coach or the principal or both? Should the principal make an announcement about the formulation of the literacy leadership team and ask for volunteers? These are all good questions that the literacy coach needs to address and, with the help of the principal, make sound choices for the school in which she or he is working.

Literacy instruction is often embraced in the primary grades (K–2), but upper elementary, middle, and high school teachers sometimes have difficulty in understanding why they, as content teachers, need to be a part of this general discussion. We believe that there are certain key personnel who must be on the team to assure the integrity of the team, and there are other personnel whose presence would be preferable if possible. If we want the literacy leadership team to make real sustainable change, the team should be made up of teachers from diverse backgrounds—from a wide range of races, ages, grade levels, and gender (Taylor & Gunter, 2006).

The teachers who must be a part of the literacy leadership team at the elementary level should come from each grade level. In addition, to be highly effective and to work for the maximum change, the team should have an administrator (preferably the principal), a counselor, as well as representatives from music, art, and physical education. If the school has an assigned speech pathologist/audiologist and school nurse, it would be advisable to have them on the team as well. The literacy coach should anchor this team.

Secondary (6–12)
Literacy Leadership Teams

At the secondary level, the team needs to have the principal, the literacy coach, as well as a member from each content area. A counselor and a representative from the vocational department as well as the technology department should also be included.

The goal is to have as many people as possible understand the importance of literacy. With some exceptions, most academic disciplines do not see the necessity to understand why we all need to be knowledgeable about literacy development. Many teachers still hold to the theory that literacy instruction is the purview of either the English/language arts teacher or a reading specialist. They see reading as a "subject" that someone else teaches. But to make real and lasting changes so that students are afforded the best possible chance to succeed, all teachers must believe that reading and writing are the underpinnings of all academic success (Craig, 2006). If students can't read or write at a certain level of proficiency, they are less likely to be successful in content area classrooms.

Summary

This chapter looked at what comprises the literacy leadership team and who should be on the team. We discussed how rules need to be generated so that the team can be successful from the start. We also examined not only the working systems that define reading but also those that define the literacy leadership team. Section One laid the foundation for understanding how we all learn. Section Two begins the discussion about the construction of the literacy leadership team. Chapter 6 takes these issues and refines them to define adaptive challenges.

When asked to form a literacy team for the elementary school, Cecilia felt uneasy. She wanted to believe that a team could work at her school, but she had worked with most of these teachers for over 15 years and knew that they thought "coaching" and professional learning were just more fads, and that if they ignored them long enough they would go away. She also believed that the upper-elementary teachers were strong-minded about their role as "literacy" teachers. They believed that if the students were struggling at this point, they should go out to special areas such as an intensive reading or learning disabilities classroom.

Cecelia knew that there was a strong group of young teachers who were eager to see school initiatives that reflected the current research—initiatives that were rooted in responsive teaching and evidenced based. These teachers were mostly from the K–3 classrooms, and they were enthusiastic about making some changes in their classroom literacy programs.

Cecelia faced the ultimate dilemma. Should she ask the veteran teachers, knowing that they didn't want to participate? Should she ask some of the newer teachers and risk alienating the veterans? Was there a way to ask some from each group that would give real balance to the team, which was her goal? How could she convince the upper-level teachers that becoming part of the team was in their (and their students') best interest?

Reflections

1. What are the real issues for Cecelia?

2. What do you think is the solution to Cecelia's dilemma?

3. What information from the chapter would help resolve the problem?

4. Develop a chart that shows how you would organize a team if you were the coach. Discuss this with your group members.

Exchange

The three teachers in the "'X-ed' change" were at a turning point in their coaching. After reading the chapter, what would you advise them to do? Think of yourself as a literacy coordinator. What could you do to help in this situation? What would you say to the administrators to help them "get on board" with their team? How might you get student representation on the team?

Assembling a Working System to Promote Forward Shifts

This is the point at which the literacy leadership team makes the theory applicable and practical for their particular school. Equipped with the theoretical understandings from Section One, the team is now ready to identify an initial adaptive challenge, investigate it, refine it, design and execute an action plan, and reflect on the action plan during and after implementation. Section One provided you with the necessary knowledge to hone and defend the team's decisions. This section provides you with the real groundwork that has to take place so that the team can tackle an adaptive challenge and improve learning and instruction.

We have chosen the term *adaptive challenge* over *area of concern* because we feel strongly that nearly all challenges that schools face can be adapted to improve and transform instruction. Realistically, all areas of concerns are always a challenge tackled by adaptations that have been generated by past experiences or new knowledge. As experienced adult learners, we know that all of life's experiences are adaptive and transformational. We propose facilitating the process by having the literacy leadership team, with the literacy coach, assemble a working system that is self-regulating, self-directing, and self-monitoring. This particular working system is recursive by nature but with forward shifts (positive change) always on the horizon. As you read through Chapters 6 through 9, keep in mind that any working system that is assembled has to be disassembled and reassembled for adaptation to take place. Knowing this is key for the success of the team and the school.

Chapter 6

Identifying Adaptive Challenges

"X-ed" Change

The principal asked Jessica, the literacy coach, if he could speak to the literacy leadership team at the first meeting. He wanted to address the school's state assessment results from the spring and talk about how they might develop a plan for working with one "adaptive challenge" for the school year. He had the adaptive challenge picked out and wanted to run it by the team to make sure they were "on board" with him. The meeting was on Wednesday.

Mr. Brandon: Thanks for letting me take the floor this afternoon. As you know, we received some pretty good test scores in the spring, and I wanted to thank you for all the hard work that you have been doing. I will talk more about that during the first faculty meeting next week, but rest assured I do appreciate the time and effort this team has been putting in. However, looking at the test scores, I see a glaring area that we can work on this year. The scores seem to indicate that our upper-elementary students aren't doing so well when it comes to making sense of a passage. They don't seem to be able to comprehend expository text. Are there any comments so far?

Jessica: Mr. Brandon, I would like to add something here. I think that looking at the students' scores across a variety of areas would be really significant in helping us formulate which plan we might want to address this year. Your "adaptive challenge" could be one of those challenges we could address, but . . .

Mr. Brandon: Thanks, Jessica, but I don't want to see us going down the "rabbit hole" where we lose our concentration. We need to concentrate our efforts this year so that when our youngsters take the test next spring, they won't have the same problem. I hope you all see the importance of this and are willing to get behind me on this.

The team members all nodded and Jessica sighed, knowing it was probably going to be a waste of the team's efforts this year. But what could she say or do? Mr. Brandon was the principal after all.

Read the following chapter, and decide what Jessica could have done prior to the meeting to help the principal understand the importance of being able to articulate what a team should work on as well as how the team can decide on which adaptive challenges are supported by assessments support as viable.

Up to this point we have reviewed and considered all the preparation that is needed to start a literacy leadership team with the active support of a knowledgeable literacy coach. We started by reviewing adult learning and developing a common language so that we could effectively and efficiently communicate about school issues at hand. Additionally, we dealt with such topics as understanding literacy as a process and its impact on analyzing data in order to make forward shifts in instruction and student learning. The term *forward shifts* is used to assist a literacy leadership team's focus, although our experience as participants and nonparticipants on many literacy leadership teams has taught us that all shifts occur in cycles that tend to energize and prompt reflection (Fullan, 2005). Previously discussed and crucial for any group work, whether at the literacy leadership team level or the classroom level with students, is setting ground rules and developing a working system so that the team can function as a group.

The working system that effective literacy leadership teams utilize to sustain and expand success begins with initially identifying some adaptive challenges (Heifetz & Linsky, 2002), followed by refining or distilling one of them, so that the team is able to investigate this specific adaptive challenge. Heifetz and Linsky (2002) draw our attention to the fact that identifying an adaptive challenge may imply that we seek solutions to current problems by utilizing known tools so that we can go beyond our current capacity in order to expand success. An adaptive challenge requires difficult learning, generates disequilibrium, and takes time. Thus, in the context of sustaining and expanding success, using the term *adaptive challenges* is certainly accurate in getting literacy leadership teams to think systemically about forward shifts in learning and instruction.

FIGURE 6.1

The Literacy Leadership Team Investigative Cycle: A Working System to Support Forward Shifts

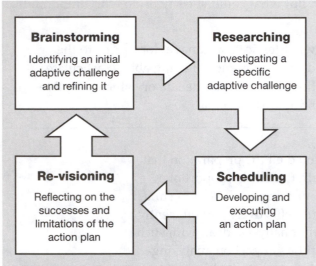

Brainstorming

Identifying an initial adaptive challenge and refining it

Researching

Investigating a specific adaptive challenge

Re-visioning

Reflecting on the successes and limitations of the action plan

Scheduling

Developing and executing an action plan

Note: Although reflection is listed under revisioning, it is a perpetual practice that needs to take place throughout the entire cycle continuously.

Once a specific adaptive challenge has been investigated, most literacy leadership teams develop and execute an action plan to impact learning and instruction. Again, we use the term *adaptive challenge* rather than *area of concern* to assist teams to focus on how we can promote forward shifts significantly to transform learning and instruction. It has been our experience that simply utilizing the word *concern* alerts the user to a problem and a negative mindset rather than a solution. Although some may accuse us of splitting hairs, we are continually challenged by the power of words and the importance of collaboratively developing a common language that does not approach educational reform from a deficit model (Johnston, 2004). After executing an action plan, the team then reorganizes itself into a reflective study group to be able to review the successes and limitations of the plan executed, and the recursive nature of the working system begins again. Figure 6.1, The Literacy Leadership Team Investigative Cycle, provides a graphic representation of a working system that effective and efficient literacy leadership teams can utilize to promote forward shifts.

As Figure 6.1 illustrates, there is no single point of entry within a system that has been developed to sustain and expand success. Even though most literacy leadership teams begin with brainstorming solutions based on data, and may follow this by researching those solutions, moving into scheduling or setting a timetable, executing an action plan, and then reflecting on the whole process, other schools may take a different route. One literacy leadership team may choose to start with scheduling, whereas another school with different strengths and needs may choose to begin by re-visioning their goal or adaptive challenge. Although some literacy leadership teams may choose to begin by brainstorming ideas to investigate, they may soon realize that after brainstorming ideas, they may want to address scheduling or researching and skip re-visioning until another cycle.

Although student learning is at the forefront of the discussion, we have to be mindful of the learning and instructional needs of the teachers themselves, since they are the experts on the students we are ultimately supporting (Lambert, 2003). Consequently, by encouraging a school culture that supports adults in learning and instruction, we are supporting an environment where students will learn and teach others as well. In turn, schools that create a safe learning and instructional environment will simultaneously be promoting flexible, critical thinking, which is necessary for forward shifts to occur.

In this chapter, we discuss using assessment and evaluation to identify initial adaptive challenges. Notice that at this point we are still referring to the adaptive challenges as "initial." *To arrive at a specific adaptive challenge, a literacy leadership team has to investigate further and co-triangulate their school data. Triangulation* is a method of assessing that cross-checks at least three discriminate ways to determine students' strengths and needs. Co-triangulating data involves bringing together information that has been cross-checked in other areas. For example, information is triangulated for individual classrooms to arrive at a truer picture of strengths and needs, and then that information is co-triangulated with information from other classrooms to determine a school's strengths and needs. In order for a literacy leadership team to arrive at a specific adaptive challenge, they must assess and evaluate strengths and needs in a variety of areas.

The literature on assessment and evaluation is sometimes confusing because many times both terms are used synonymously. We define *assessment* as documenting strengths and needs. *Evaluation,* in the context of literacy instruction, is utilizing documented assessment to determine the next steps based on current understanding of literacy processing. We strongly feel that the only good assessments are the ones that are consistently and systematically observed and documented over time. This does not dismiss informal observations that classroom teachers make on a daily basis, but it does emphasize that those informal observations be documented in order for them to be revisited.

Using Assessment to Guide Investigations

As a literacy leadership team begins to organize itself with the support of a literacy coach, the team needs to retool itself to rethink of assessments from a dual perspective in order to identify an initial adaptive challenge or challenges. The dual purpose that we're referring to is thinking of assessment as *assessment for* learning and *assessment of* learning. This means that members of the literacy leadership team have to adjust how they think about assessment guiding instruction in order to dig deeper and arrive at a specific adaptive challenge rather than going off and running on an initial challenge. For example, after reviewing a state standardized test on reading, *an assessment of learning,* many times a group will get together and formulate a conclusion about what to investigate, let's say vocabulary development, because on the surface it may appear that the majority of the students were identified as needing that particular support. Yet, further investigations may lead the group to arrive at a more concrete issue that can support classroom teachers in honing their instructional practices so that they can truly make a difference. After more research, the team may come to the realization that vocabulary is probably the surface issue, but the deep structure underlying the problem is the students' understanding about using affixes in content-specific assignments. The school, in turn, may now decide to develop an action plan or timetable outlining how students will be taught and exposed to prefixes and suffixes of Greek and Latin origins. This fine-tuning, compounded with understanding why we assess, will ultimately lead to successful implementation of instructional practices at the school and classroom levels.

Kellough and Kellough (1999) argue that the importance of assessment cannot be overemphasized and outline seven reasons for assessing:

1. To assist student learning
2. To ascertain students' strengths and needs
3. To gauge the effectiveness of an instructional practice
4. To inventory and enhance curriculum
5. To upgrade learning and instruction
6. To document change over time and assist in informed decision making
7. To update parents on their children's progress

In addition to understanding why we assess, we have adopted and adapted 10 principles identified by the American Association for Higher Education (Banta et al., 1996) that should serve literacy coaches and literacy leadership teams as a guide for effective and efficient use of assessment to inform learning and instruction. These nine adapted guiding principles were originally created by the American Association for Higher Education with a tenth proposed by Banta and colleagues (1996):

1. Student assessment starts with what is valued in education.
2. Effective assessment takes into account that learning is multifaceted, integrated, and manifested in performance over time.
3. Assessment works best when there are clearly defined purposes for programmatic improvement.

4. Effective and efficient assessment needs to be formative and summative.

5. Ongoing assessment works best rather than intermittent assessment.

6. Assessment is more likely to promote forward shifts when diversity is taken into account.

7. To make an impact, assessment needs to be used to investigate adaptive challenges.

8. Assessment is effective and efficient when it is used to sustain and expand success systemically.

9. To support learning and instruction, assessment needs to guide instruction.

10. A safe and supportive environment needs to be in place for assessment to be effective.

Initially, most literacy leadership teams look at data that qualify as assessment of learning. After thorough and careful review, the discussion should go further and look into cross-checking or triangulating the information with assessment for learning, since effective assessment is multifaceted, ongoing, and integrated. Think of it as a vertical and horizontal review of assessment where vertical is assessment *of learning* and horizontal is assessment *for learning*. Figure 6.2 illustrates vertical and horizontal assessments with examples of each provided for further study and to prompt an in-depth discussion on the importance of not relying on one source of data to make an informed decision. Table 6.1 is to be illustrative of a variety of assessments and it is certainly not meant to be exhaustive. Your own school, district, and state will more than likely use some of the assessments listed as well as others. The point is that both types of assessments are necessary before a true evaluation can be made by the literacy leadership team.

FIGURE 6.2

Using Vertical and Horizontal Assessment to Define Adaptive Challenges

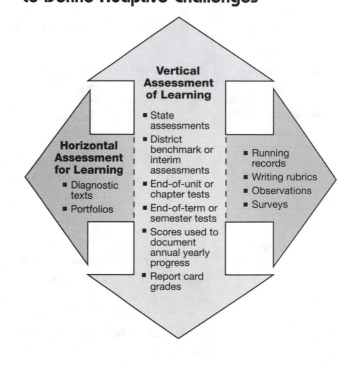

Vertical Assessment of Learning
- State assessments
- District benchmark or interim assessments
- End-of-unit or chapter tests
- End-of-term or semester tests
- Scores used to document annual yearly progress
- Report card grades

Horizontal Assessment for Learning
- Diagnostic texts
- Portfolios

- Running records
- Writing rubrics
- Observations
- Surveys

TABLE 6.1

Assessment Tools: Levels of Use and Purpose

Assessment Tool	Level of Use	Purpose of Tool
Standardized Tests	State, District, School	Measures students' learning against others in the same grade level against a national norm. Tests are developed by testing companies.
Criterion-Referenced Tests	District, School	Measures students' learning based on information learned. Tests are prepared by publishers or teachers.
Chapter Tests	School, District	Measures students' learning of specific information learned in a particular chapter of a textbook or novel.
Spelling Tests	School, District	Measures students' learning of specific words at any given grade level. Prepared either from a district-developed list, a school list, or a publisher's list.
Writing Samples	School, District	Collected from students and compiled from samples of writing in various content areas.
Journals	School, District	Writing samples from various content areas. Journals can be dialogue or individual.
Running Records	School, District	Analyzes students' oral reading and what strategic actions students are using or neglecting during reading.
Fluency Analysis	School, District	Data gathered from reading passages that determine the time, tenor, and tempo students use while reading.
Informal Reading Inventories/Surveys	School	Data gathered from surveys that determine students' critical understanding of key features of a leveled passage.
Performance Based	School	Students are evaluated on a performance based on a literacy experience (e.g., demonstrating comprehension by playing a role from a novel).

Earlier we addressed this issue using the terms *static* and *dynamic* assessment (Dixson-Krauss, 1996). We consider static assessment to be assessment of learning, whereas dynamic assessment is assessment for learning. Merely looking at one type of assessment to the exclusion of the other will more than likely provide a literacy leadership team with inaccurate and skewed information.

The literacy leadership team has to consider reviewing data that take into account how students are doing in comparison to other students and how students are processing the information being presented to them. To sustain and expand success in literacy instruction, we have to look at student products and how students are processing information. Many times, this is easier said than done. Time and communal knowledge are usually hurdles. Time to administer and analyze with some degree of consensus (communal knowledge) can be a challenge. These hurdles can just as easily be overcome by the literacy leadership team developing a common language and constantly working toward a clearer understanding of how students process information.

At the elementary level, it means that the literacy leadership team identifies an initial adaptive challenge by using firsthand assessments that are required by schools, districts, and states. Although good information can be obtained from district- and state-required assessments, this information alone will be insufficient to narrow an initial adaptive challenge to a specific one that can guide instruction regardless of the grade level. In the primary grades, a simple timed horizontal test of phonics, phonemic awareness, or fluency produces insufficient data to amplify instruction and make forward shifts in literacy instruction. Generally, these types of tests have the potential to assist teachers in grouping students and selecting materials, but they do not tell teachers what strategic activities students are using and which ones they are neglecting to use and need to be taught. Although it may be a good starting point, further assessments need to be investigated to make an informed decision to truly guide literacy instruction with a goal of promoting strategic literacy learners. Initial adaptive challenges seldom guide instruction effectively or efficiently. In many cases, *literacy leadership teams that seek solutions for initial adaptive challenges without attempting to get to the root of the issue rarely sustain or expand success.* Quick fixes seldom last or can be used to further learning (Allington & Walmsley, 2007). Further investigation is always necessary and critical.

In middle and high school, standardized tests are inadequate in creating powerful literacy lessons for students. We are not saying that standardized tests need to be abolished nor are we bashing standardized tests. What we are saying is that standardized tests alone are not enough to make a positive impact on literacy instruc- tion. As we have stated, standardized tests are *assessments of learning*. They have to be triangulated with *assessments for learning*.

With adolescent students having so much of their processing rapid and metacognitive, student/teacher conversations, as well as student writing samples, have to be considered in all content areas as well as their standardized tests, so that we will be able to make powerful instructional decisions. Of course, in order for assessments of learning to be used effectively, a clear understanding of literacy processing is essential. Without this clear understanding of literacy processing by teachers, literacy coaches, and literacy leadership teams, even assessments for learning can be used to misguide instruction regardless of the best of intentions (Clay, 2001; Gillion, 2004). Think of how many times you have seen well-intentioned language arts teachers focus instruction on the skill of identifying the main idea, sequencing, or recognizing cause and effect based on a sole source of static assessment without evaluating how such a skill can assist students in processing information. Assessment without evaluation is the equivalent of driving a car without a steering wheel. You'll get somewhere—but who knows where?

Using Evaluation to Guide Practice

Teachers use assessment to let their students know how they are doing. In business, it would be taking the inventory. We use evaluation to gauge how our teaching is being received. This is what we need to run the business. Evaluation is when our knowledge of theory, practice, and experience interplay to prompt us into making informed decisions to improve learning and instruction. In this case, theory is not only determining what is going on in the students' heads but it is also determining how to interact with what we think is going on in the students' heads.

For this to occur, we return to our mantra that teachers, literacy coaches, and literacy leadership teams need to have a strong foundation on how students process information for assessment to have any value in recognizing and addressing adaptive challenges. Without this clear understanding, adaptive challenges become areas of concern or simply a surface theme of significance to be replaced during the next fashionable wave of instructional practices. We have seen many good instructional practices go by the wayside because the theoretical understanding was not present to either explain or defend a particular practice. For example, many of us use graphic organizers to support student learning. Some of us have used them more successfully than others. Based on a number of conversations with classroom colleagues, it is evident that the teachers who have a solid theoretical understanding of literacy processing are the ones that teach students to use graphic organizers successfully. Consequently, those students are the ones who embrace this instructional practice as a learning opportunity and eventually internalize it and use it as a self-initiated strategic activity to remember or to clarify when engaged in literate enterprises. Yet, a solid theoretical understanding of literacy processing alone will not suffice if a repertoire of instructional practices is not known or investigated for future reference. *When a theory remains only at the theoretical level, it eventually becomes a moot point or considered a passing fad.* In order for a theory to be useful, it has to get to the practical level. Moreover, for theory to get to a practical level, assessment and evaluation have to be employed. By evaluating assessments, literacy coaches and literacy leadership teams bring to the table their collective knowledge and experiences as another source of information to cross-check or triangulate static and dynamic assessment. *Assessment for the sake of assessment is worthless if not evaluated and used to improve learning and instruction.*

Like assessment, evaluation needs to be ongoing, developing, and evolving if it is to be a productive learning and instructional experience. Additionally, like assessment, evaluation must be multifaceted to ensure that no stone is left unturned when it comes to improving learning and instruction. Evaluation should also be collaborative and relevant. Many of our colleagues prefer to use the term *authentic,* but we argue that what is authentic for one person in a given situation may not be for another person in a similar situation. Moreover, it may not even be authentic to the same person in a different situation. Consequently, we prefer to use the term *relevant. Authenticity* usually describes objects, whereas *relevancy* defines actions. In our minds, *relevant* seems to be a more precise term when addressing issues of learning and instruction. Once again, it may seem that we're splitting hairs over terminology, but we cannot overstress the importance of the words we choose to communicate with students, colleagues, administrators, politicians, and parents (Johnston, 2004).

Summary

In this chapter we investigated the importance of assessment and evaluation as a starting point for literacy leadership teams to sustain and expand success by identifying adaptive challenges. Additionally, we introduced the term *adaptive challenges* to replace the commonly used term of *area of concern* to frame the team's thinking to seek solutions in a proactive manner. By addressing adaptive challenges, the literacy leadership team, with guidance from the literacy coach, is more likely to engage in activities that will promote expanding success to improve learning and instruction.

By cross-checking summative and formative assessment, tempered with conventional wisdom and experience, appropriate evaluations can be utilized to seek solutions for adaptive challenges. Looking at data from the dual perspective of assessment of learning and assessment for learning, or, as we referred to it, vertical and horizontal assessment, can serve literacy leadership teams as a platform to begin investigating how best to improve learning and instruction for everyone at a school. We encourage literacy leadership teams to copy Table 6.1 and utilize it during a variety of meetings with colleagues, administrators, and parents to highlight the necessity of using a variety of assessment instruments before making any decision on how to tackle adaptive challenges. Without viewing assessment as a multifaceted inventory of learning and instruction, ineffective and inefficient data collection will more than likely emerge putting a temporary halt to forward shifts at a time when forward shifts are critical. It merits repeating that the list of assessments listed in Table 6.1 is an illustrative list of assessments and is certainly far from being exhaustive. Utilizing Table 6.1 can serve literacy leadership teams by framing the need for short-term, mid-term, and long-term planning of assessment and evaluation. A copy of the table can serve a team as a reminder of the need to cross-check vertical and horizontal assessments in order to make logical and rational evaluations based on evidence.

In the next chapter, we will look at how literacy leadership teams can use the professional literature to refine, limit, and investigate adaptive challenges in order to move forward in a reasonable and manageable time. Although detours will be inevitable, efforts need to be made to stay on track. To assist teams in staying the course, we will briefly review a variety of specific instructional practices that can be employed to address adaptive challenges in learning and instruction within a literacy framework or program (a specific series of instructional practices orchestrated to support independent and flexible learners).

LIBRETTO

Janice called the team together to start examining the adaptive challenges that they thought would be worthwhile to engage in for the school year. As the literacy coach and team leader, she wanted members to understand that they needed to be able to articulate their position to the administration so that the team would receive support. The challenge she was proposing was based on something she learned at her coaches' summer institute.

While at the institute Janice learned about developing an assessment tool that each teacher could use in the classroom to inform her or his practice. This tool is a "survey" style of assessment that asks students *what* they were learning, *how* they were learning, and *which* instructional practices the teacher was using that were effective and not effective. Janice thought that the teachers in her middle school would really like this assessment tool and that the team could refine it to a four- or five-question survey that teachers could easily fit into their weekly schedules.

Janice explained this all to the team and was stunned by their blank stares and silence. Had she missed something? What weren't they seeing about this wonderful new approach to getting vital information from students?

Reflections

1. What was Janice's main goal and why wasn't it well received?

2. From the chapter, what information about the way we use assessment was Janice not connecting to?

3. Janice's "new tool" was what kind of assessment—"for" learning or "of" learning?

4. What should the team do to help Janice rethink her position?

Exchange

You have read the "'X-ed' Change," the chapter, and the libretto. In this "'X-ed' Change," the principal violated several rules for building consensus as well as not defining an adaptive challenge. What would you ask the principal about his position that would lead him to understand the importance of taking on adaptive challenges—ones that support the needs of the school as a unit? How could you incorporate his "challenge" into one that that the team could use and support? What could the team do to help him make decisions that support long-term, lasting change?

Chapter 7

Investigating an Adaptive Challenge

"X-ed" Change

The literacy leadership team was asked to look at the ways the state standards could be implemented more effectively in the classroom, especially during the literacy block. Basically, they were to look at the assessments to see what teachers were using effectively and what could be improved upon.

After poring over hundreds of documents, they concluded that there must be a wide range of ways in which teachers were teaching reading and writing, and that there were several teachers who provided only skills and drills reading instruction. The team decided that the literacy coach should make time to visit each classroom where this was happening and try to get the teachers to see how they could improve their test scores with a broader range of instructional practices.

The coach emailed one teacher, Mrs. Rainey, and made an appointment to meet with her during her planning period.

Debra: Mrs. Rainey, thanks so much for agreeing to meet with me. The literacy leadership team has been asked to look at our assessments from the spring and we noticed that when you teach in your literacy block you use only drill activities from the reading workbook. Have you thought about using different techniques, such as shared and guided reading?

Mrs. Rainey: No, I didn't want to go back and take those workshops. They didn't look like they would really work all of the time, and I know that the drill exercises do. It's just a fluke that my scores are down. I'm doing all I can, but I appreciate you coming by.

Debra: Is there anything you think you will be changing about your literacy block for this year?

Mrs. Rainey: As I said, I like the way I teach the students now. I'm happy with the workbook, and the parents like to see the homework I send home. I don't see anything else to do, but thanks for stopping by.

Debra realized that she wasn't going to move Mrs. Rainey this way, and thanked her for her time. Leaving the classroom, Debra wondered how she could have handled it so that Mrs. Rainey wanted not only to make changes but also understand why they were so necessary.

Read the chapter and the libretto and think of ways in which the information from this chapter could have helped Debra with the challenges presented by Mrs. Rainey. How could this "'X-ed' Change" be turned into an effective "change" agent?

In the previous chapter we talked a lot about the importance of *assessment of learning* as well as *assessment for learning*. We looked at ways in which literacy leadership teams can avoid taking a snapshot of the assessments and perhaps miss an important adaptive challenge that should be addressed. The main purpose for discussing and evaluating assessment of learning and assessment for learning is to initially identify adaptive challenges that need to be investigated and refined into a specific adaptive challenge that the literacy leadership team can investigate further, keeping the benefits on the forefront. Dismissing particular benefits from the start has the potential to misguide literacy leadership teams. In this case, always on the forefront needs to be the frame of mind of what's in it for the students that teachers will find manageable.

In this chapter we look at how to find that all-important adaptive challenge and how to use professional resources and literature to help explore the adaptive challenge in depth. Since the purpose for refining an adaptive challenge is to put a plan in action, we will also review some instructional practices teachers can employ to support students' learning. The select instructional practices we have chosen to review are meant to work as a system for learning and instruction. Each instructional practice is to be viewed as an opportunity for teachers to observe, assess, and evaluate learning in a variety of contexts so that we can promote flexible and independent learning behaviors. We do not intend for this chapter to serve as an in-depth study of the individual instructional practices. Rather, it is meant as a bird's-eye view to prompt the literacy leadership team to investigate the instructional practices further, using resources beyond this text. Bear with us as we use the menu metaphor once again. Think of this chapter as a menu, much like the ones you see in restaurants. Food items are listed, but ingredients and preparation are usually omitted. Yet, for successful implementation of an action plan to improve learning and instruction, literacy leadership teams need to find instructional practices to tackle adaptive challenges effectively and efficiently that teachers need to work in their classrooms.

Using Assessment Tools to Connect to Instructional Practice

One of the first things a literacy leadership team should do to begin the process of finding an appropriate adaptive challenge is to examine the various types of assessment, both static and dynamic, that impact their schools and their students, and that instructional practices are supported by the use of these types of assessments. *Static assessments* are those that state an outcome over time, such as norm-referenced (standardized) tests and criterion-referenced (textbook) tests. *Dynamic assessments* would be those types that are gathered while students are in the process of reading or writing. Some examples of these are reading records or writing samples.

Table 7.1 provides a brief list of assessments, the category the assessment belongs in, and what instructional practice can be employed supported by the assessment. It should serve as a springboard for literacy leadership team members, and is in no way an exhaustive list of assessments or instructional practices. You may have additional ones that you could add to the chart. The table represents various types of tools we have used when assessing and evaluating the literacy experience of our students and how teachers can validate their instructional practices with the appropriate assessment. For example, when we do a shared reading and a read-aloud with the students, not only are we modeling the "voice" of a reader but we are also helping the students see how we decode words to construct meaning. When the students engage in independent reading time with teacher support, they are practicing the strategic activities that they will need to be successful critical learners. Likewise, when they engage in writing enterprises, they are developing skills and strategic activities that are necessary for the teacher to assess, so that she or he can amplify instruction to assist accelerating their literacy development.

TABLE 7.1

Dynamic and Static Assessments

Assessment Tool	Type	Instructional Practice Connection
Standardized Tests	Static	All practices
Criterion-referenced tests	Static	All practices
Chapter tests	Static	Interactive read-aloud, shared, guided, interactive, independent reading
Spelling tests	Dynamic	Interactive spelling instruction
Writing samples	Dynamic	Modeled, collaborative, interactive, independent writing, interactive editing
Journals	Dynamic	Modeled, collaborative, interactive, independent writing, interactive editing
Running records	Dynamic	Interactive read-aloud, shared, guided, interactive, independent reading
Fluency analyses	Dynamic	Shared, guided, interactive, independent reading
Informal reading inventories/Surveys	Dynamic	Interactive read aloud, shared, guided, interactive, independent reading
Performance-based tests	Dynamic	All practices

Your literacy leadership team may decide that they want to choose teaching sequencing as an adaptive challenge as a key feature of teaching literacy instead of looking at the students' overall literacy development. If this is the case, the following things may be of benefit:

- What kinds of approaches (whole group, small group, workstations, etc.) does the teacher use?
- What instructional practices (read-aloud, guided reading, literature discussion, etc.) of a comprehensive literacy approach are evident? Which ones are not? How does the teacher assess literacy development in her or his classroom?
- What does the teacher understand about literacy as a process?
- Does the teacher use observation in the classroom?

As a member of the literacy leadership team, it is your obligation to help teacher colleagues understand that you are not "grading" them. Rather, you are there as an "invited observer" to help them investigate and employ appropriate instructional practices that support forward shifts in learning and instruction. In order for this investigation to take place, we have to rely on past and current professional literature.

Using Professional Literature

Once the team has decided on an adaptive challenge to study, it is important that the team has the appropriate professional resources to support it. One of the literacy leadership team's responsibilities in to ensure that there are appropriate financial resources budgeted so that each team member has access to professional books, journals, and online resources. This is one reason why it is absolutely critical that principals be active members of the literacy leadership team, since ultimately the school's finance and budget are their responsibility. Additionally, the literacy coach as the lead learner should be able to provide a list and brief introductions to texts that support the various topics under consideration.

Another critical member of the literacy leadership team is the media specialist. She or he can provide a space in the media center to house the various texts the team might use throughout the year, as well as journals that will be of help to them as they investigate, broaden, and deepen their understandings of literacy as a process. In some schools, media specialists create a "niche" or a "den" for the literacy leadership team to meet and study. This place is usually furnished with comfortable seating and is well stocked with professional books, journals, and magazines. Internet access in the area is a must, for literacy leadership team members need to have the most up-to-date research at their fingertips when meeting.

When the team determines what texts or text they want to use, the team can choose from a variety of ways to respond to the text and when. The first way they might approach the study is by each member reading the entire text and then coming together in one of the meetings to discuss and respond. Another way is to divide the text into sections and every fourth week come together to discuss. If the majority of the members in the study group are new to the team, it might be best to have chapters read for each meeting and then take some time during the meeting to ask the members to respond. If the team has been together for awhile, it might be a good idea to have an online reader's response to the text, utilizing either email or the chatroom concept.

The point to remember is that it is important that each literacy leadership team member understand the importance of refining his or her knowledge by reading, writing, talking, and thinking about the theoretical underpinnings that support literacy growth. In this way, the team will be able to match instructional practices with the theory and research, know when teaching is effective and when it is not, and what to do to make appropriate forward shifts.

Instructional Practices to Employ

For the literacy leadership team to sustain and expand success, they should investigate and engage in instructional practices that support a comprehensive literacy approach that is culturally sensitive and diversified. The following instructional practices are presented as possibilities for literacy leadership teams to investigate further. There are certainly others, and the literacy leadership team should decide which of these are relevant to them.

Language Experience Approach

Based on the work of Sylvia Ashton-Warner (1965), this highly supportive instructional practice is used by teachers to show students the connection between spoken language and print. Although used primarily in the early grades, it is an excellent instructional practice to use with English language learners and low-progress readers. Although you might have students who speak various dialects and who don't use traditional standard English, depending on the teacher's purpose, it is important to write down the words as they are spoken. The language experience approach acknowledges the child seeing the importance of his or her language and how spoken language "looks" in print. As students progress in language development you will be able to adjust your teaching to meet the challenges of acquiring conventional semantic, syntactic, and graphophonic structures that support a self-extending system.

Whether a shared experience is created or the child's personal experience is used, the teacher listens and writes down what the students say so that it may be reread once it is printed. The language experience approach shows the students the importance of their words and provides them with reading material. Moreover, if the teacher makes corrections either structural or conceptual, the child may have difficulty "reading" the text (Gunning, 2004). As Cunningham and Allington (1998) remind us, "If language experience is being used with an individual child to help the child understand what reading and writing are and that the child can write and read what he or she can say, then the child's exact words must be written down. To do anything else will hopelessly confuse the child about the very things you are trying to clarify by using individual language experience" (p. 92).

The language experience approach is a highly supportive instructional practice in promoting literacy acquisition. It should not be a stand-alone practice in any literacy program; rather, it should be used in combination with other instructional practices to provide rich literacy experiences for students.

Read-Aloud

This instructional practice of a literacy program ensures that students are exposed to the strategic activities that readers use when they are engaging with text. The teacher models the appropriate tone, tenor, and tempo while reading. The students are able to discern appropriate fluency while the teacher is modeling. They listen to the story as the teacher shows how to engage with the text and how to construct meaning from print. From time to time the teacher may stop and highlight specific strategic activities such as questioning and predicting to further the students' literacy experience. Used primarily in the early grades, the read-aloud practice is also a good way to show low-progress readers and English language learners what readers do. It can also be used to show middle and secondary students what readers do when they engage in various genres such as those in the content areas.

What does a read-aloud lesson look like? We have found that when we employ the read-aloud as an instructional practice, we need to be knowledgeable about the book we choose. Even though we acknowledge that ultimately a read-aloud is meant to engage students in a sensual experience with text, we must have a book that is age and developmentally appropriate and one that provides us the opportunity to promote the strategic activities we want students to use flexibly and independently. We often hear from teachers that read-alouds shouldn't be used after the elementary years. We believe this is anything but true. There are still ample opportunities to use this instructional practice with middle and high school students. Given the appropriate text, students of all ages love to be read to. Think of how many times you have read a newspaper article or a particular page from a book to a friend or colleague. That is a read-aloud. Of course, the operative words are *relevancy* and *appropriateness.* The same applies for students regardless of whether they are in elementary, middle, or high school.

Another important feature is to consider a variety of ways in which the students can respond to the text. This can be through small-group discussion, reenactment of the story, a retelling of the story, or a journal entry. Whatever way you choose, it must match the purpose for using the read-aloud in the first place.

Interactive Read-Aloud

Like a read-aloud, an interactive read-aloud starts from the premise of modeling what readers do when they engage in a text. The interactive read-aloud takes it a bit further in that it asks the person doing the reading to engage the listeners by prompting brief discussions at specific points during the reading. The teacher may start by questioning what the text will be about, what kinds of concepts will be encountered, or what unique language might be involved in this book. She or he then reads the text, stopping to predict and anticipate where the author is going with the story, or what the characters are going to be doing. After reading on for a while, the teacher again stops to clarify any of the issues that might have been brought up in questioning. Then, after reading the designated amount of pages, she or he summarizes what has been read by retelling. In this interactive read-aloud, the teacher shows students what readers do "in their heads" when processing what is being read. At certain intervals (predetermined) the teacher asks the students to discuss what they think is going on in the text.

As in a traditional read-aloud, an interactive read-aloud is ultimately employed as an instructional practice to engage students with print. Although a powerful instructional practice, we have to share a word of caution when using an interactive read aloud: Too many interruptions of the story for the sake of teaching may destroy experiencing the author's intent. Thus, employing an interactive read-aloud as an instructional practice is a delicate dance between teaching and entertaining.

Shared Reading

Based on the work of Don Holdaway (1979), shared reading has been described as a classroom version of a bedtime story or eyes on print with voice support. Shared reading is about the teacher reading *with* the students (Mooney, 1990). The experience is one in which the teacher as well as the students engages with the text. In the lower elementary grades, the teacher uses an enlarged text, such as a big book or chart. She or he reads and points as the children watch and read along. During the initial read through, the students may or may not read aloud with the teacher, but during subsequent readings, the students are expected to participate and join in on the parts of the story they know. With this age group, the teacher usually uses large books that are highly predictable, rhythmic, and have lots of repetition.

In the upper elementary, middle, and high school grades, the teacher may use an enlarged text on an overhead projector or students may have a copy of the reading material at their desks and follow along as the teacher reads. At this level of instruction, shared reading sounds very much like choral reading. Whereas the read-aloud experience allows students to see what readers do when they read, the shared reading experience asks students to participate in what readers do by taking on some of the responsibility for reading. It scaffolds the students while they are reading and provides instruction in strategic activities that the teacher demonstrates. Experienced teachers utilize shared reading with a specific focus lesson.

Guided Reading

Guided reading is reading by the students. The teacher does not engage in the reading of the text when conducting a guided reading lesson. This is the time when students are provided reading materials that they can read with approximately 90 to 94 percent accuracy. During a guided reading lesson, teachers observe students as they read and provide support when necessary. As readers become more proficient over time, guided reading evolves and may resemble a literature discussion group with teacher support.

The guided reading experience puts children who have "similar needs" together in one group. For the lower grades, it provides small-group instruction with a text that is challenging but not outside of the children's capabilities, and it aids the students in both comprehension and word development. Experienced teachers who implement guided reading on a daily basis generally have in place the following procedural sequence:

■ *Introducing the text:* Teachers provide the main idea of the text and introduce one or two challenging vocabulary words, creating a sense of anticipation that prompts students to want to read the text. It is a book talk that teases the reader to read.

■ *Reading the text:* After the teacher introduces the book so the students are somewhat familiar with the text they will read, the teacher asks them to read the text. In the early grades, the students may read aloud while the teacher listens to how students are processing print. When a child encounters difficulty, the teacher prompts the student to seek solutions strategically, prompting for flexibility and independence. In the upper grades, the teacher may ask the students to read to themselves and tap individual students to whisper what they are reading to gauge how they are processing print.

■ *Discussing the text:* After reading the text, the teacher asks the students to discuss what they have read. She or he revisits any vocabulary with which the students continue to experience difficulties. Through this discussion, the teacher can determine what concepts need clarification.

- *Teaching for strategic activity:* After the discussion, the teacher determines what strategic activity she or he needs to revisit and reinforce. (Revisiting Chapter 4 is beneficial.)

- *Extending meaning (optional):* Based on the discussion and the strategic activity selected, the teacher may want to extend the lesson by asking the students to respond in a journal or act out a certain part of the text. Lyons and Pinnell (2001) call this "extensions to help students make their understandings explicit" (p. 38).

- *Word work (optional):* Depending on the difficulty level of the text and the needs of the students, the teacher may decide that the group (or some members in the group) need additional word study. Using whiteboards or letter tiles, the teacher helps the students investigate how words work.

In one of our guided reading lessons with a group of fifth-graders, the group had been reading Laura Ingalls Wilder's *Little House on the Prairie*. The group hadn't read from the text in a few days, so a storyboard exercise was used to have them "revisit" previous chapters. Eight box diagrams were drawn on the board and the students were asked to give three or four events from each chapter. After this review, questions were asked about where they thought the story was going next, what the characters might be doing, and so on. Based on what they placed in the storyboard, the students were also asked to determine the next "sequence of events," prompting them to process the story by predicting and anticipating. The students were instructed to begin reading the chapter and to raise their hands if they had difficulty.

After several minutes, one student raised his hand. The student said he was reading along and didn't know the word *bodice* (he pronounced it "bo dice"). The teacher asked what he had been reading about before the word occurred in the text. He said that the mother was sewing something for one of the girls. The teacher asked the student what the first part of the word sounded like, and he replied "bod." From that, he made the leap to "bod ice" and then finally to "bodice" for the correct pronunciation. He also was able to figure out that the mother was sewing the "body of the dress." He happily returned to the text comfortable that he had discovered for himself (through appropriate prompting) how to figure out new words he wasn't sure of.

This is a very important function of the guided reading experience. Students need to develop those strategic activities that help them function as independent readers. When they approximate, search, confirm, or reject their approximations, they are developing what Clay (2001) calls a "self-improving" system.

Independent Reading with Teacher Support

It sounds cliché but it really is true—we learn to read by reading, not really by watching others read or listening to them all the time. Independent reading time is when students get to "ride the bike." When we provide support during this "ride," we are the "training wheels." We listen and provide scaffolding when we are needed, but otherwise the reading time is the time the students invest with the text on their own. This time is usually spent reading silently, although very young students usually read aloud. During independent reading with teacher support, students read books at their independent level of instruction, although sometimes they select texts that are just a little bit higher than their actual instructional level because they are interested in the topic. Interest is a powerful motivator to support students' reading. While the students are reading independently, the teacher is roving the room, either listening in or generating brief conversations to gauge how the students are doing.

Modeled Writing

When you read aloud to your students, you are showing them what good readers do with texts—both familiar and unfamiliar. The same is true for modeled writing. When you model writing as a process, you are showing them what writers do to get a message down on paper to entertain, inform, or persuade.

Modeling writing calls for the teacher to write something "on the fly," not having a "prepared script" that has been edited for all mistakes. We do this because students need to see the steps along the way—not just the finished product. We have all had experiences where a teacher showed us a writing sample and then sent us off to "mimic" it. Remember feeling helpless as you tried to understand how those perfectly formed words and sentences got on that page? By modeling, teachers show how they choose words and sentences, how they organize their thoughts, and how they edit for conventions.

In modeled writing, we talk out loud about the processes that happen in our heads. We share how we choose certain words, how we ask questions of ourselves about structure, or organization, and how we decide where we go next. Modeled writing is not a time for teachers to test students' editing skills. When modeled writing is utilized as an instructional practice, teachers do not make intentional mistakes for students to hunt and find. Teachers want to model what proficient writers do and proficient writers do not make intentional mistakes.

Interactive Writing

Interactive writing is a hybrid of shared writing and the language experience approach, where the "pen is shared" by the teacher and the students (McCarrier, Fountas, & Pinnell, 1999). An instructional practice employed in the primary grades, interactive writing is a highly supportive activity that supports students through writing as a process while working toward independence and flexibility. A general sequence of instruction for interactive writing is (1) composing a message as a result of the students and teacher brainstorming or rehearsing what they are going to write; (2) constructing a message, actually putting pen on paper by students and teacher, with the teacher supplying information the students are not able to provide at this given point in their educational career; and (3) rereading the written text for a variety of reasons (such as clarifying, editing, or revising). The major difference between this instructional practice and other supportive writing practices is the so-called sharing of the pen between students and teacher.

Collaborative Writing

Collaborative writing is an instructional practice designed around students and teacher working together to write. Generally, the teacher scribes for the students as they brainstorm what they want to include in their story. The teacher may start off with the topic sentence and then let the students work from there. She or he asks questions as they explore various literary elements, and points out areas that might need revisiting after they are through with their draft.

Although collaborative writing has also been called interactive writing, we distinguish the two instructional practices. Based on our experiences, collaborative writing is interactive writing grown up. A major difference between the two is that in *collaborative writing,* either the teacher or a student "holds the pen," whereas in *interactive writing,* the "pen is shared" (McCarrier, Fountas, & Pinnell, 1999). Since collaborative writing is an instructional practice used with students who have mastered the conventions of print, it is employed to focus on refining the craft of writing by emphasizing focus, organization, and elaboration.

Guided Writing

In guided writing, the teacher brings a group of students together who need to work on some specific feature of writing—usually something that she or he has taught during more supportive instructional practices such as modeled writing, language experience, or collaborative writing. The teacher directs the students to work on this issue as she or he watches, providing guidance as they work through their writing. Similar to guided reading, guided writing is small-group writing instruction by the students with teacher support. Guided writing is usually implemented in classrooms that have adopted a writing workshop approach to writing, where everyone in the class is usually writing about a self-selected topic and engaging in focused discussions on elaborating or improving the writing. The teacher's role in guided writing is to monitor and support students in their writing endeavors. A guided writing lesson follows this sequence: (1) introduce a particular piece of writing to serve as a model or anchor, highlighting a particular aspect of the writing; (2) students write independently, with the teacher intervening and prompting when necessary; and (3) students engage in a writer's talk about their writing, or the next step in their writing.

Interactive Editing

Interactive editing is a daily oral language activity where a specific example is used to focus on a particular aspect of print. Here, the teacher works with the students as they try their hands with editing while talking. It is through these rich editorial talks that students learn the language of writers to refine their own writing. They learn to address such issues as appropriate word choice, spelling, good sentence structure, and other grammatical aspects of writing while engaged in constructive dialogue about the writing. In an interactive edit lesson, the teacher creates a sentence or paragraph with specific mistakes that he or she uses to highlight particular teaching points for the students to use in their own writing. Most teachers are used to the concept of daily oral language activities. Interactive editing is similar to daily oral language activity with the exception that based on years of classroom observations, daily oral language activities have become a sit-in-your-seat-writing-activity involving copying or a handout with minimal oral language activity.

Independent Writing with Teacher Support

Independent writing time is very important to students so that they can invest time in writing for their own purposes. This is the time when they can explore writing in various genres, and can practice the skills and strategic activities you have been teaching. As in most of the writing instructional practices we have reviewed thus far, independent writing is an integral part of a classroom that has adopted a writer's workshop approach. Although it may have a different look and feel from classroom to classroom, independent writing with teacher support scaffolds students in realizing the reciprocity between reading and writing and how one endeavor supports the development of the other. Generally, the culminating experience for this writing time is a writer's talk, when students share and discuss their writing.

Interactive Spelling Instruction

No one will discount the importance of spelling instruction. Interactive spelling instruction focuses students on the importance of spelling as a courtesy to readers. In an interactive spelling lesson, students engage in a variety of activities that require reading, writing, talking, and thinking. Spelling words are generally derived from the students' writing or what they are currently reading and focus on how to strategically determine conventional spelling. An interactive spelling lesson may involve having students do word sorts (open and closed) and using spelling games (e.g., Hang Man), crossword puzzles, and word searches. Like traditional spelling instruction, interactive spelling instruction does include a test at some point so that the teacher can determine the next steps in spelling instruction. Although unlike a traditional word list spelling test, a test of interactive spelling instruction is generally in the form of sentence dictation involving self-assessment with peer and teacher support.

Interactive Vocabulary Study

Interactive vocabulary study is a hybrid instructional practice that borrows from shared reading and collaborative writing. During an interactive vocabulary study, the emphasis is on oral language development with a focus on how words work. For example, an interactive vocabulary study will never focus on a particular set of words; rather, it will focus on words that have a similar Greek origin or Latin origin. Words chosen for an interactive vocabulary study may focus on a particular prefix or suffix. This type of instruction aims to develop students' lexical working system (refer to Chapter 4 in this text).

Literature Discussion Groups

As in the other approaches we have mentioned, the students' experiences must be relevant and purposeful. Instead of just asking them to read and write a book report, they should have a genuine reaction and response to the texts they are reading. Literature discussion groups allow this to happen.

Usually, a literature discussion group is comprised of a community that "shares" a text or texts with a common theme, much as a group of adults would do. It can take place in whole or small groups, and can be either formal or informal (Gunning, 2004). Unlike the traditional study group, where the teacher asks directed, prescribed questions, the literature discussion group is prompted to interpret the text they have read and defend their interpretation by using the text. Alvermann (1996) suggests that these types of discussion groups promote a deeper understanding and a broader comprehension of the material being read.

To develop an effective literature discussion group, the teacher must model the appropriate behavior the students need to employ to be able to get the most from the discussion. She or he must scaffold this experience so that students can see how to return to the discussion when they get off task, or how to resolve conflicts when members of the group disagree.

Literature discussion groups can be centered on one text, or it can be centered on a theme. At all grade levels, the purpose is to be able to respond to text in a personal and pleasing way, to be able to think deeply about the subject matter, and to show once again the connection between the reader and the writer.

Summary

We have reviewed how assessment and evaluation can be used to investigate adaptive challenges and which instructional practices can be employed to tackle such adaptive challenges to promote forward shifts in learning and instruction. These types of assessments can support a literacy leadership team in addressing adaptive challenges that involve a broad range of instructional practices within the classroom. In order to assist the literacy leadership team to refine identified adaptive challenges that can be tackled effectively and efficiently, we proposed that the team needs a working knowledge of a variety of instructional practices that can be implemented to promote forward shifts in learning and instruction. With that end in mind, we provided brief explanations of a variety of instructional practices that the team may choose to investigate further.

The intent of this book is to guide literacy leadership teams to sustain and expand success. To provide a full list of instructional practices and descriptions is beyond the goal and scope of this book. We do, however, encourage literacy leadership teams to accept this chapter as food for thought and as a challenge to investigate further in order to support the students and teachers who will be impacted by the team's decisions. Although brief, we listed a variety of ways in which reading and writing can be presented to the students—ways that are purposeful and that will have life-long meaning to them. In Chapter 8, we will continue our journey in assisting you to keep refining an adaptive challenge to increase the likelihood of sustaining and expanding success. We will show how to develop a focus based on literacy processing in order to improve learning and instruction.

Juan was a new literacy coach and had only been in the classroom five years prior to this new role. He wanted to make a strong first impression on the literacy leadership team he would be working with, so he decided that he would get all the test scores from the previous school year and map out the areas that needed serious investigation. He read them carefully and decided that there were several teachers (and one on the literacy leadership team) that could use some "help."

At the first team meeting, Juan told his colleagues about what he had discovered and then passed out worksheets for them to sign up for coaching sessions. Listed on the sheet were such areas as "writers' workshop," "interactive word study," "using dynamic assessment in the classroom," and "using round-robin reading groups more effectively." He asked his colleagues to sign up and list how they would go about studying the designated topics. Without really saying why, he specifically asked the "teacher who needed the help" to choose a coaching session she would like to work on with him. At the end of the session, Juan asked the team members to let him know as soon as possible how they would present this information to the teachers needing the "help."

Reflections

1. What has Juan missed that reading this chapter would have helped him?

2. What would be your response to this type of team meeting?

3. As the district coordinator, how would you council Juan to be a more effective team leader?

Exchange

You have read the "'X-ed' Change," the chapter, and the libretto. As a literacy leadership team member, what could you do to help Debra understand the issues she really needs to address in order to be more effective in her role? What could she have said to Mrs. Rainey that would be more beneficial to her as a classroom teacher? What are the pitfalls that Debra should avoid so that she doesn't have the same reaction from other teachers to whom she is really trying to give help?

Chapter 8

Refining an Adaptive Challenge and Developing an Action Plan

"X-ed" Change

Wanda tried to picture what her team would do when she told them that the district wanted the team to study literacy—specifically, lesson planning. Most of the teachers on her team had been writing lesson plans for 15-plus years each. They had strong ideas about the direction they wanted the team to move toward so that they could work effectively with the teachers in their grade level. As elementary teachers, they were especially sensitive to being "told" what was "good practice" and what wasn't. Nevertheless, Wanda knew she had to follow the district's mandates or risk having the literacy leadership team lose their support.

Wanda decided to call a meeting and let her colleagues know so that they could plan accordingly. The meeting was called for Monday afternoon.

Wanda: Hi everyone. Thanks for coming on such short notice.

Adam: Wanda, we're glad to be here because we have heard rumors that the administration is going to require that we study lesson planning this year. We already know how to write lessons and don't see this as a productive use of our time.

Wanda: Hold on a minute, Adam. It's a little more complicated than just writing lesson plans. The district needs us to take a strong look at how literacy is being used in each lesson in the content areas. They believe that many of us are forgetting that literacy reaches across all subject areas and underpins everything students do. We all know that reading and writing are the foundation of learning in the content areas. But the district administrators think there are several teachers—especially in our school—who don't understand what we are talking about. They want us to collect samples of each teacher's lessons, study what they are doing, and then go in and work with them to revise their plans so that they match the district policies.

Katrina: Don't you think teachers are going to resent this? Don't you see this as a put-down to their experience in the classroom?

Wanda: Well, I guess I think that it doesn't really matter, but that you will have to somehow position yourselves so that they see you as credible and will therefore want you to work with them. I think you are all strong mentors and can provide modeling that works well with their students.

Ray: Well, I for one would like to say that I am not happy about this at all, and I will be considering dropping off of the team. The fifth-grade teachers that I work with will be up in arms, even though I think they really trust me.

Wanda: Well, Ray, I hope this doesn't mean that you drop out, but if you decide to, let me know soon so I can get a replacement. If there aren't any other issues, we can adjourn. I will be sending around a template of the format the district wants us to use. Look for it in your box on Wednesday and make any notes you want and bring it with you to the next meeting on Monday. Thanks, everyone.

Read the chapter and the libretto. Decide what the real issues are and come up with a plan that could turn this "'X-ed' change" into meaningful change that supports the role of the literacy leadership team.

In years of working with various literacy leadership teams, we have found that refining an adaptive challenge and focusing on using vertical and horizontal assessment of learning and instruction for literacy processing is a very difficult task. Part of the difficulty in addressing the issue is twofold and arises because many times teams have not taken the time to develop a common language and do not have a clear understanding of literacy learning as a process so that they can tackle a specific adaptive challenge. This is where we have found that a knowledgeable literacy coach becomes an invaluable member of the team, and the concept of the literacy coach as a lead learner comes to fruition. In other words, adaptive challenges cannot be tackled with only surface knowledge; rather, deep understanding is required to get to the root of the challenge. *Utilizing a knowledgeable literacy coach as the conduit for professional learning can assist the literacy leadership team in achieving the necessary deep understanding.*

We have found that to refine an adaptive challenge, the literacy leadership team needs to:

- Develop a common language.
- Have a clear understanding of literacy learning as a process.
- Be aware of past and current research.
- Have the ability to identify the need for future research.
- Possess a working knowledge of instructional practices that can be implemented.
- Understand the students' strengths and needs.
- Understand the teachers' strengths and needs.
- Develop a menu of possible literacy focus lessons that teachers can use.
- Develop a focus based on literacy processing.
- Create a short-term and a long-term plan for implementation.
- Design a literacy framework that supports all students and accounts for learning over time in grades K–12 with built-in safety nets at all grade levels.

Developing a Focus Based on Literacy Learning as a Process

Throughout this book the points listed here have been addressed in greater detail than is intended for this chapter. In this chapter we want to investigate the importance of developing a focus to tackle an adaptive challenge based on literacy as a process. Revisiting Chapter 4 in this text will certainly support literacy leadership teams in refocusing on literacy as a process. Without this clear understanding, we are convinced that any analysis of data will more than likely be misinterpreted, even with the best intentions. We do have to warn you, though, that analyzing any literacy assessment and figuring out how to address it within the concept of assembling working systems is in and of itself a challenge. Yet, it has to be put on the table and dissected to develop a common language and to truly impact learning and instruction for forward shifts.

One of the easiest ways that we have found to guide literacy leadership teams in tackling adaptive challenges by focusing on literacy as a process is for the team to generate a list of possible focus lessons about concepts or information that students need to learn. At this point, it could even be a list of behavioral objectives or state/district benchmarks or standards. Read and consider the list of some nonspecific focus lessons that we have collected over time (see Figure 8.1). After reviewing the list (you can certainly create your own) as a team or in smaller groups, use Figure 8.2 to tackle each focus-lesson and reword it so that each one reflects literacy as a process more specifically. The charts shown in Figures 8.3 and 8.4 can serve you as a guide in rewording your focus-lesson or lessons so that they reflect addressing learning and instruction to assist students in developing a self-extending system for learning. Not only do we encourage literacy leadership teams to engage in rewording focus-lessons to refine adaptive challenges, but this particular activity of listing and rewording focus lessons is an excellent endeavor for literacy coaches to engage in with classroom teachers to articulate, defend, and implement instructional practices that will promote intentional instruction.

FIGURE 8.1

Examples of Nonspecific Focus-Lessons

1. Create interest, set purpose, build background knowledge, and preteach vocabulary.
2. Build background knowledge and model reading strategies during teacher read-aloud (think-aloud)—questioning, making connections, and cooperative comprehension.
3. Identify words in context, know the meaning, and expand student vocabulary.
4. Students will be able to demonstrate use of eighth-grade vocabulary, understand text, and see relevancy.
5. Students will be able to identify a word in context, know its meaning, and use it in their vocabulary.
6. Students will be able to identify unfamiliar vocabulary words by indicating the meaning of various prefixes, suffixes, and root words.
7. Using the graphic organizer provided, students will be able to make an inference.
8. Students will demonstrate knowledge of the vocabulary words in Chapter 2.
9. Students will demonstrate knowledge of the characters introduced in Chapter 1 by completing a graphic organizer.
10. Actively focus on relationships among words, use vocabulary terms in conversation and writing, and expand definitions through a variety of elaborations.
11. Make connections between our personal lives and the text we read in order to enhance understanding.
12. Apply the comprehension strategies of predicting, visualizing, making analogies, and recognizing confusion, and fix up strategies to comprehend text.
13. Use, define, and a apply list of set vocabulary.
14. Use word-attack skills and "test taking" strategies to successfully work a cloze.
15. Make and verify predictions using the text and background knowledge.

FIGURE 8.2

Developing a Specific Focus-Lesson Based on Literacy as a Process Activity

1. In groups, select focus-lessons from the list given in Figure 8.1.

2. Review Chapter 4 and "Possible Focus Lessons for Reading" chart.

3. Discuss and decide how to reword focus-lessons to reflect the language of reading/writing as a process based on the charts (Figures 8.3 and 8.4).

4. Write the reworded focus-lessons below.

5. Share focus-lessons with the group for discussion.

Focus-lesson:

_____

_____

_____

Focus-lesson:

_____

_____

_____

Focus-lesson:

_____

_____

_____

Focus-lesson:

_____

_____

_____

Focus-lesson:

_____

_____

_____

FIGURE 8.3

Possible Focus-Lessons for Reading

- Predicting and anticipating using meaning (main idea)
- Predicting and using language structures (grammar, oral language pattern)
- Predicting and using print (initial, medial, or final consonants, vowels)
- Predicting using lexical information (prefixes, suffixes, root/base words, Latin origins, etc.)
- Predicting and anticipating using pragmatic information (author's intent, genre)
- Predicting and anticipating using schematic information (prior knowledge, context)
- Checking predictions with meaning (Does it make sense?)
- Checking predictions with language structures (Does it sound right?)
- Checking predictions with print (Does it look right?)
- Checking predictions with lexical information (Is there a part of the word I know?)
- Checking predictions with pragmatic information (Is that what the author meant?)
- Checking predictions with schematic information (Is there something I know about that?)
- Searching further using meaning (What else do I know that makes sense?)
- Searching further using language structures (What else do I know to make it sound right?)
- Searching further using print (What else do I know to make it look right?)

- Searching further using lexical information (What other words or part do I know like that?)
- Searching further using pragmatic information (What else could the author mean?)
- Searching further using schematic information (What else do I know about this?)
- Self-correcting using meaning (Does that make sense?)
- Self-correcting using language structures (Does that sound right?)
- Self-correcting using print (Does that look right?)
- Self-correcting using lexical information (Is there a part of the word I know?)
- Self-correcting using pragmatic information (Is that what the author meant?)
- Self-correcting using schematic information (Is there something I know about that?)
- Rereading to confirm predictions
- Rereading to check predictions
- Rereading to search further at difficulty
- Rereading to self-correct
- Rereading for phrasing to support fluency
- Rereading to …
- Assembling or integrating working systems for comprehending
- Assembling working systems flexibly
- Clarifying to confirm or reject predictions
- Summarizing to clarify or remember
- Self-questioning to expand meaning

Early Reading Behaviors (Clay, 2001)
- Cross-checking sources of information
- One-to-one word matching

- Left-to-right progression of print
- Return sweep progression of print
- Locating known and unknown words

105

FIGURE 8.4

Possible Focus-Lessons for Writing

- Forming intentions by using graphic organizers
- Forming intentions by using models (genres as mentor texts)
- Forming intentions by using personal experiences
- Forming intentions based on audience
- Forming intentions for expository text
- Forming intentions for innovating text
- Forming intentions by using resources (informational material)
- Constructing expository text
- Constructing narrative text
- Constructing persuasive text
- Constructing poetry
- Constructing letters (business, personal)
- Constructing lists
- Constructing ...
- Editing for meaning
- Editing for visual information or print (spelling)
- Editing for grammar or language structures (periods, capitalization, etc.)
- Editing for lexical information or word choice (ed, ing, est, etc.)

- Editing for genre structures (expository, narrative, etc.)
- Editing for accuracy of information
- Editing for handwriting
- Editing for ...
- Proofreading for meaning
- Proofreading for language structure
- Proofreading for spelling
- Proofreading for lexical information
- Proofreading for pragmatic information
- Proofreading to confirm intentions
- Proofreading to check intentions
- Proofreading for ...
- Using multiple resources for forming intentions
- Using multiple resources for composing
- Using multiple resources for editing
- Using multiple resources flexibly
- Using multiple sources for scribing (pen, pencil, computer, etc.)
- Clarifying to confirm intentions
- Summarizing to confirm intentions
- Self-questioning to confirm or clarify intentions

Early Writing Behaviors

- Hearing and recording sounds in sequence
- Spacing
- Left-to-right progression of print (word level or sentence level)
- Return sweep progression of print
- Conventional spelling of basic sight words (the, to, is, etc.)

For example, the first focus-lesson listed (in Figure 8.1) states "Create interest, set purpose, build background knowledge, and preteach vocabulary." Let's dissect this one together to illustrate our line of thinking and the conversations that need to be taking place in order to address a specific adaptive challenge effectively and efficiently based on how students process information. At first glance, there are too many teaching points for effective and efficient learning and instruction to occur. There are actually four teaching points or focus-lessons stated. Based on many conversations with teachers across the country, experienced, effective, and efficient educators generally limit teaching points to one or two. Think of your own past teaching experiences. Many of us have had the experience of overteaching too many concepts. The results usually are abysmal because students can process only so much new information at a given time. Sometimes by overteaching, we may be confusing more than we are assisting student learning. We need to start by rethinking and refining our focus-lessons in order for the lessons to be a powerful learning experience. For the sake of argument and to illustrate our thinking, we are going to choose preteaching vocabulary. Simply listing "preteaching vocabulary" is not specific enough for a literacy leadership team to take on the concept as an adaptive challenge to present to classroom teachers. A quick glance at Figure 8.3 will assist you in focusing on preteaching vocabulary in a more targeted manner to improve learning and instruction. As in any learning experience, there is always more than one choice. As Marie Clay (1998) stated, "We all take a different path to a common outcome." Consider the following focus-lessons that have been reworded to reflect reading as a process by using the term *preteaching vocabulary*:

■ Preteaching vocabulary to support predicting and anticipating when reading

■ Preteaching vocabulary to support checking predictions

■ Preteaching vocabulary to support searching further at difficulty

■ Preteaching vocabulary to support self-correcting when it doesn't make sense

Each one of the focus-lessons reframes "preteaching vocabulary," a teacher-directed activity, to what readers (students) need to do in order for them to become self-regulating, self-directing, and self-extending learners.

When identifying adaptive challenges, the literacy leadership team, with support from a knowledgeable literacy coach, needs to go through this exercise of rewording before presenting a menu of possible solutions to teacher colleagues. We have found that when literacy leadership teams, with the best of intentions, skip this investigative rewording of adaptive challenges, the solutions to the adaptive challenge identified become a sequence of activities with no relevance to student learning. *Adaptive challenges have to be reworded and transformed from specific teacher behavior (e.g., preteaching vocabulary) to specific student behaviors (e.g., preteaching vocabulary to support predicting and anticipating when reading) if forward shifts in learning and instruction are to occur.*

An alternative manner to reword an adaptive challenge is to consider the benefits to student learning and rewording the adaptive challenge to reflect the benefits to the students. By considering the benefits to the students, the literacy leadership team will begin to rethink and reword adaptive challenges to promote forward shifts in learning and instruction that promote self-regulating, self-directing, and self-extending learners. Once the literacy leadership team has refined an adaptive challenge that reflects literacy learning as a process, the team's next step is to develop an action plan for implementation.

Developing an Action Plan for Intentional Literacy Instruction

An action plan for intentional literacy instruction has to address an adaptive challenge or challenges through practical steps that are measurable over time while simultaneously taking into account the people and resources necessary for implementation. Successful implementation of an action plan is dependent on the literacy leadership team's cross-functional collaboration with teacher colleagues inside and outside of the team. These cross-functional collaborative relationships serve as interlocks. These interlocks do not necessarily appear on an action plan, but evolve as subcommittees to keep the literacy leadership team informed and to ensure effective implementation. These interlocking relationships involve giving and receiving in collaborative action research to refine even further an adaptive challenge.

An action plan for intentional literacy instruction is a document that states an adaptive challenge and identifies all the necessary action steps required to tackle the adaptive challenge. Action steps are the *who, what, and when* of implementation. Effective action plans for intentional literacy instruction will include:

- Specific adaptive challenge
- Short-term and long-term assessments
- Grade levels impacted

- Resources
- Action steps on a timetable
- Alternative action steps based on interim assessment and reflection

Figure 8.5 is a template of an action plan for intentional literacy instruction to support a literacy leadership team. *The action plan needs to be relevant and clear based on cotriangulated data that considers not only past and present performance but future needs as well.* For this to occur, the literacy leadership team needs to develop an action plan for intentional literacy instruction that is:

- Simple
- Takes into account teachers and students
- Designed in achievable increments
- Specific in roles and responsibilities
- Flexible

Executing an Action Plan

After carefully refining an adaptive challenge to reflect literacy learning as a process and developing an action plan, the literacy leadership team's next step is to consider executing the action plan that supports teacher colleagues in engaging in intentional instruction to promote forward shifts in literacy learning. This is where a literacy coach's expertise and knowledge of andragogy and pedagogy meet to support the literacy leadership team in determining the best possible route to sustain and expand success in learning and instruction for teachers and students.

In implementing an action plan for intentional literacy instruction, the literacy leadership team and the literacy coach have to consider the professional learning opportunities that need to be facilitated by the literacy coach to support teacher colleagues in implementing the action plan over time. It will be beneficial for the team and the literacy coach to preview Chapter 10 about utilizing the literacy coach. They need to consider how literacy coaching on a continuum (Figure 10.2) will support the literacy coach in assisting teacher colleagues in implementing instructional practices that tackle the specific adaptive challenge that was identified based on the action plan for intentional literacy instruction.

FIGURE 8.5

Action Plan for Intentional Literacy Instruction

Specific adaptive challenge identified:
Short-term and long-term assessments:
Grade levels impacted:
Resources needed:
Action steps/timetable:
Alternative action steps:
Reflections:

Summary

The task of defining a specific adaptive challenge as it relates to literacy processing involves a literacy leadership team learning about how students process information and how teachers need to interact with what is occurring during that processing. It is a complex act of analysis that has to be investigated over time with hard data and conversation. *Seldom will a literacy leadership team arrive at a specific adaptive challenge in one sitting or session.* Even when an adaptive challenge is identified fairly quickly, it is still necessary for the team to develop a focus based on literacy processing in order for the team to decide what instructional practices will be most effective and efficient in tackling the challenge.

Once the literacy leadership team has determined a specific adaptive challenge and developed a focus based on literacy processing, it is the team's task to design an action plan for intentional literacy instruction to promote forward shifts in learning. After crafting the action plan, the team and the literacy coach have to address the best possible support system to put in place to ensure implementation success with teacher colleagues. This chapter in combination with others in this book and *The Literacy Coach: Guiding in the Right Direction* (Puig & Froelich, 2007) will support the literacy coach in taking on the role of lead-learner by revisiting the multifunctional job of the literacy coach on a continuum of professional learning. Chapter 9 will address the next steps after developing and implementing an action plan for intentional literacy instruction through the development of study groups and reflection on the implementation of the action plan in order to sustain and expand success.

LIBRETTO

Yasmine really loved teaching sixth-grade mathematics. She thought there was nothing better than getting the students to see that they were really capable of working complex math and that it could be fun at the same time. She liked the fact that mathematics was orderly and that the students knew that if they listened carefully there wasn't much they couldn't do. So imagine her surprise when the school's "reading" coach emailed her to set up a meeting about her "lessons." The meeting was set for Tuesday during her planning.

Yasmine: Hi Ellis. I haven't seen you all year. What's up?

Ellis: Well, Yasmine, as you know, we have been given very specific mandates by the district to examine the literacy plans each teacher is using. Your plans were mentioned to me as ones that could use a little "polish."

Yasmine: What do you mean? You're a reading coach, and I teach mathematics.

Ellis: Well, that's just the point. I am the "literacy" coach, which means that I work with teachers in all subject areas, but as you know, before I took this job, I was a math teacher, too. What we need to do is set a time when I can come into your classroom and observe how you deliver your lessons and what literacy skills you are utilizing during the lesson. How does that sound to you?

Yasmine: To tell you the truth, Ellis, it sounds terrible. I am perfectly happy with my lessons, how they are delivered, and the results I get from the students. My test scores are adequate each year, so I don't see the problem.

Ellis: I see your point, but this has been decided by the principal, and, well, I'm going to have to show them some paperwork sooner or later, so it might as well be sooner. I have an article here that I would like you to read before I come in next week. What day would be best for you?

Yasmine: I guess Wednesday would be good. We will be starting a new unit and you can see how I introduce the concepts to the students.

Ellis: Great Yasmine. I'll see you on Wednesday, and don't forget to give that article a good once-over.

Reflections

1. What issues did the literacy coach ignore that could have helped him better prepare for his meeting with Yasmine?

2. What were the key points that Ellis should have addressed?

3. What was Yasmine's real reason for not wanting this "intrusion" into her classroom?

4. What are the responsibilities of a literacy coach that Ellis has overlooked?

Exchange

You have read the "'X-ed' Change," the chapter, and the libretto. What would you and your team do to resolve the problems Wanda created? What could the team do to turn this into a truly significant exchange—one that meets the demands of the district but respects the needs of the team?

Chapter 9

Developing a Study Group and Reflecting on the Action Plan

"X-ed" Change

Barbara had really looked forward to being chosen to serve on the literacy leadership team. She had heard so many wonderful things from her friend Jessie about how the teams chose literacy issues to work on for a school year. She looked forward to taking part in the study groups, and she had some good ideas about articles they could read and discuss in the group. But after the first meeting, she made a date with her friend to talk about what she thought were going to be some real problems with her team, especially two of her teammates.

Barbara: Jessie, I am so disappointed in our team meeting. After you raved about how great your experience was last year, I was really looking forward to my time on the team. But the first meeting was a royal disaster. Some members came in late, some talked over the coach, and some were just not interested in anything she had to say. She started out asking us to prioritize our concerns about literacy in the school for the year. She asked us to write a little about what we would like to explore during our meetings. That's when a couple of people started in on how they couldn't believe we were going to spend a year talking about reading and writing. The coach tried to explain that there was more to literacy exploration than just reading and writing, but these two people just shut her down. She didn't know what to do, so she just pushed ahead with our interests.

Jessie: In our meetings the coach came in with several suggestions and we listed the order in which we wanted to work on them.

Barbara: Not this coach. She had just started to talk about things the district wanted the teams to look at when the two last members of the team came strolling in talking about how awful bus duty was. I thought if you were on the literacy leadership team you were supposed to be excused from bus duty for the year. So after they finally sat down, the coach brought this up. They turned a little red, mumbled something, and when we took our break, they left and didn't come back. What have I gotten myself into?

Read the chapter, the libretto, and reflections and discuss what Jessie can say that would make Barbara feel more comfortable working with her team members.

Once a literacy leadership team has a specific adaptive challenge to investigate, it is the team's responsibility to reorganize themselves into a professional study group to review the current literature on the subject to enable the group to reflect on the action plan they had originally developed. Additionally, as we have stated previously, we strongly believe that part of the job of a literacy coach is to be a "lead learner" within the context of the literacy leadership team. What this means is that it is the literacy coach's responsibility to organize the team as a study group and serve as a resource for materials to study. As stated in *The Literacy Coach: Guiding in the Right Direction* (Puig & Froelich, 2007), facilitating study groups is part of a literacy coach's responsibility in order to support job-embedded professional learning. In this chapter we will review and make suggestions to assist literacy leadership teams in transforming themselves into a professional study group in order to help themselves sustain and expand success at school with the support of a knowledgeable literacy coach.

Learning in groups is not a new concept. Groups have been studying together for hundreds of years. The modern-day practice of working in cooperative groups was created by W. T. Harris, a nineteenth-century educator (*Teacher Today*, 2003). He helped students achieve rapid promotion through group work. He believed that students would, in fact, prefer to work in groups rather than the isolated, assigned seating way that most schools use.

In our work with literacy coaches and literacy leadership teams, we have found that the same principles and guidelines that apply to cooperative learning groups apply to study groups. There are five elements that define cooperative group learning according to Johnson and Johnson (1999):

- Positive interdependence
- Face-to-face promotive interaction
- Individual and group accountability

- Interpersonal and small group skill development
- Group processing

Johnson and Johnson (1999) further explain that *positive interdependence* is the notion that all group members are in this together. They must be reliant on each other to be successful. Although we firmly believe that transforming the literacy leadership team into a professional study group to tackle an adaptive challenge, it is also important that each individual member of the study group is personally held accountable for contributing to the group's collective knowledge on the subject. *Face-to-face promotive interaction* is when each member assists the other in learning and provides appropriate generative responses. By providing generative responses, members of the literacy leadership team engage in dialogic conversations to clarify and promote deeper understanding of the adaptive challenge being studied. *Individual and group accountability* is the concept that each member must be an active participant and must contribute to the group. To ensure that all members accept individual and group responsibility for the study, Chapter 5 provides you with guidelines for setting ground rules. When your language is clear and explicit, there will be fewer misinterpretations about accountability and responsibility not only to the group but also to the school and students (Puig & Froelich, 2007). *Interpersonal and small group skill development* is when the group builds trust and communication through shared decision making and conflict resolution. The team will be strong when the literacy coach as a lead learner understands the dynamics of group learning and his or her role as the lead. *Group processing* is the time members reflect on what they have accomplished and how effectively the group is working together.

Oftentimes teachers think of their days as isolated and lonely. They don't have time to collaborate or to reflect with their peers (Puig & Froelich, 2007). Since literacy leadership teams are made up primarily of classroom teachers, being a member of a study group will promote a culture of collegiality and help them voice interests and concerns in a safe environment. As a study group, the literacy leadership team needs to have similar goals and see the real purpose for the group. The study group should help the team members "expand and further their own knowledge base," allowing them to be "flexible, self-regulating and self-extending learners" (Puig & Froelich, 2007).

Although there are many reasons for creating study groups, the purpose of a study group for the literacy leadership team is centered on investigating, refining, and solution seeking for a specific adaptive challenge. It should provide literacy leadership team members the opportunity to read, reflect, discuss, and integrate new concepts and ideas to improve instruction (Allen, 2006). The team should not see the group as a place to just generate "new ideas" for classroom teachers to implement. It should also be a place where literacy leadership team members can integrate research and theory into practice. To be effective, the team should have knowledgeable members that are admired and respected by peers.

Birchak and colleagues (1998) think that there are two things the study group *should not* be: a place for a staff meeting and a place for an in-service meeting.

There are also some things that the literacy leadership teams *should* promote. It should be a place where volunteering is a requirement. No teacher should be forced to be on a literacy leadership team, much less in a study group, when benefits are not acknowledged. It should be a place that helps team members not only build a community of learners but a place that challenges the members to think about literacy and instruction in ways that they haven't thought of before. Finally, a strong study group integrates research, theory, and practice. The team members realize that studying an adaptive challenge is about more than finding those "fun" activities. The team members need to know why those "activities" work, and when they don't, why not. Only by having a sound theoretical understanding of literacy learning as a process can this occur; otherwise literacy instruction will be hit or miss (Clay, 2002; Puig & Froelich, 2007).

This chapter examines the dynamics of the group, looks at what happens in the group, and shows how topics are chosen and how resources are found. We begin with the role of the literacy coach as a lead learner.

The Literacy Coach

In helping the literacy leadership team develop effectiveness, it is important that the lead learner helps the team understand the roles that each must play. It has been our experience that a knowledgeable literacy coach is generally the best person to serve as a conduit of information for the literacy leadership team, leading us to conclude that a knowledgeable literacy coach should serve as the lead learner guiding others on the team. With that end in mind, the literacy coach must (adapted from Tomlinson, 2001):

- Coach the members so that they understand their roles and responsibilities.
- Make certain that the members know what is expected of them.
- Provide challenges without frustrations.
- Build group assignments that require and benefit from shared knowledge and collaboration.

- Provide an exit strategy for those members who feel, for whatever reason, that they cannot meet the demands of the group or assignments.

- Make herself or himself available for conferring, suggesting, and directing as needed by the team members.

- Let the team members know what each task will be and the approximate time that it will take to complete.

It is worth noting that group work calls for less direction by a leader—in this case, the literacy coach. It requires that the literacy coach help establish the group dynamics. She or he should help facilitate the group by finding resources, organizing the initial meetings, and participating in choosing an appropriate adaptive challenge to study, but then should act in an advisory role whenever possible. Always supportive, the literacy coach, as a lead learner, needs to let others take the lead during the group meetings as much as possible. One way to do this is to have a "rotating" spokesperson for each meeting. By rotating responsibility, the literacy coach is promoting a safe environment where capacity building is encouraged and honored. *It is only through capacity building that success can be sustained and expanded.*

Reaching Consensus

How does the team choose what to study? How are topics elicited and then decided on? There are many ways to establish a list of topics, and we generally believe that for the team to be successful and for team members to want to continue meeting with the other members, it is best if the whole team comes to a consensus about what they want to study. Of course, on the forefront should always be improving learning and instruction. No one will argue with that goal. Conflicts generally arise when a member shares how he or she thinks learning and instruction can be improved. Since all teachers come to the table with their own set of experiences and knowledge about learning and instruction, reaching consensus is critical. Birchak and colleagues (1998) list several ways in which the team can determine the most relevant topic for study to assist in reaching consensus and move forward. One way can be determined by district mandates. If your district has decided to change literacy programs (a published sequence of materials), or develop a new assessment tool, then it might be that will be the chosen topic as it applies to your school and students.

Another way to find a topic is at the school level. The literacy leadership team could decide to investigate a topic that the faculty has listed as "critical" for change based on student data. They could look at such things as how the practice of grading portfolios is working, or how the school supports new teachers. These topics could take the "inquiry format," where the team actually creates a collaborative action research plan following the *literacy leadership team investigative cycle* illustrated in Figure 6.1.

The team may decide to study some theoretical aspect of curriculum or literacy acquisition. Based on student data, the team could decide to look at finding a way to see how their science curriculum could be coupled with the language arts curriculum, for example. This would require that the team read broadly about science and language arts to see what curriculum experts recommend for this approach. The team might also have to investigate scheduling as well as issues that concern grade-level appropriateness.

It's important to understand that the topic should always reflect the needs of the students, and team members should be encouraged to bring their experiences, knowledge, and hard data to the team. Literacy leadership team members should feel safe to ask questions and to say that they aren't knowledgeable about a topic. All team members need to feel that the topic is not imposed on them. Since an adaptive challenge is based on student data, all team members should be able to say, "I can learn a lot from this" rather than "Someone else wants me to learn about this." It is really important that there is an honest expectation (one of the conditions for learning) that the topic will be beneficial and that the team members want to learn about it. For this reason, it is essential that adaptive challenges or topics studied always be based on cross-checked or co-triangulated student data. Consensus is seldom achieved based on one source of information. Multiple resources have to be investigated. Horizontal and vertical assessments have to be evaluated.

Selecting Resources

After evaluating vertical and horizontal assessments, literacy leadership team members face the daunting task of deciding not only what adaptive challenge to study but also what materials and resources are relevant and obtainable. The literacy coach, serving as a lead learner, can have a brainstorming meeting as the first meeting to determine the topic. She or he could then put together a list of possible books or articles that the team could use. Brainstorming is generally an initial stage in the literacy leadership team investigative cycle (refer to Figure 6.1).

Another way is to have the members identify what areas of the topic they are most interested in based on student data and research possible resources they will read. Then the team comes together and charts what these are and how they will coordinate with other members' resources.

They could also decide that one person has more dynamic resources to start the study group and they would then focus their attention on that book, article, or topic of adaptive challenge. The following is an illustrative list of recommendations where you can find materials and resources to support a study group:

- The International Reading Association website
- The National Council of Teachers of English website
- Publishers that promote professional learning and have professional learning materials
- The National Council of Teachers of Mathematics website
- The National Council of Teachers of Science website
- The Association of Supervision and Curriculum Development website
- The National Staff Development Council website

Additionally, you can ask your media specialist to help provide assistance in locating appropriate resources that will help you achieve the goals that the team has established.

Planning for the research your team will do will require a concerted effort from each member of the team. Figure 9.1 looks at the various components that you might consider before deciding on what collaborative action research to undertake. We suggest that the team take some time to fill it out before the first meeting. Utilizing horizontal and vertical assessments, there may be other topics that are unique to your school setting that you might want to consider and present to the team as well. Team members can then discuss what plan they have chosen and with the other members try to reach consensus. This will save time and energy for all team members.

Reflecting on the Action Plan

Throughout the entire literacy leadership team investigative cycle, reflection plays a different role at each stage that will impact the team's future direction. Part of the task of the team in transforming itself into a study group is to seek information that will prompt reflection and alternative ways of thinking to find solutions for adaptive challenges. If forward shifts are to occur, reflection within each stage of the entire literacy leadership team investigative cycle is necessary. We have found that the collaborative nature of literacy leadership teams is a perfect and safe setting for literacy coaches, teachers, and administrators to engage in true dialogic conversations that promote reflection even long after a meeting has ended.

FIGURE 9.1

Planning for Collaborative Action Research

Directions: Make a list from most important (1) to least important (5) of the things you would like to study for this academic year. List what you think would be appropriate resources, the personnel needed to complete the study, and any money and equipment needed.

What to Study	Resources Needed	Personnel Needed	Budget Needed	Equipment Needed
1.				
2.				
3.				
4.				
5.				

6. Other Characteristics for Consideration

In the elementary school, our experience with literacy leadership teams has shown us that study groups have spawned professional reflection with a focus always remaining on student learning. On many occasions, we have found that teachers begin to question literacy coaches and administrators about possible professional learning opportunities based on information that team members shared with their peers. When literacy leadership teams are adopted at a school site along with a literacy coach as a model for reform or change to improve student learning, schools become empowered to reflect and create their own changes.

At the middle and high school levels, reflection on the action plan that is intended to be implemented becomes far more time sensitive compared to their elementary counterpart. This is even more so at the high school level, where students are approaching the end of their school careers, excluding college. Reflecting on the action plan for teams in middle school and high school has to go beyond focusing on literacy as a process and address learning as a process across content areas. We are not saying that we ignore literacy processing as a viable means of improving instruction. We are saying that we need to reflect on whatever action plan we put in place, since most students in middle school and high school will not be there as long as elementary students.

Think about this: Students are in elementary school for at least six years, seven if you have pre-kindergarten. At the middle and high school levels, the majority of students are generally there for four years. That is a two- to three-year difference that can make or break a student's academic career. Do literacy leadership teams need to reflect and promote reflection? *Yes*. This is especially true in middle school and high school, where adolescents (they are still children) are coming with physical and societal growing pains.

Summary

This chapter examined how study groups are structured, and how groups can choose topics of interest that support the literacy goals of the team as well as those that will help create a stronger learning environment for their students. We looked at how resources can be selected and provided an illustrative list of organizations that provide materials that support professional learning. Chapter 10 will take this information and show how the literacy leadership team and the literacy coach can develop job-embedded professional learning using the team study approach.

Jim was beginning his second year on his school's literacy leadership team and he was excited to be a part of a new study group. He really wanted to study how his students could get more out of the reading experience. Jim had read a lot over the summer and thought his group would perhaps want to investigate literature circles because they all were trying to move away from round-robin reading groups.

The first team meeting of the year, however, did not go as he had anticipated. The literacy coach thanked everyone for returning for another year on the team and began to discuss the formation of the year's study groups. Unlike last year, the coach let everyone know right up front that the district had "directed" them to look at one of three topics. They could study discipline issues, they could explore a new "basal" series, or they could look at how they could help their students increase fluency rates.

Jim was really disappointed and it showed on his face. The literacy coach apologized to the team and said that "sometimes district mandates had to take precedence over the needs of the group." Jim had a true dilemma. Should he ask to be released from his commitment to the team, and try to find some colleagues that would like to form a different group just to study what he was interested in? He knew he didn't have enough free time to do both groups. He hated to give up on the team, but they weren't going to be studying anything he was interested in. He knew he really had to spend some time thinking through this carefully.

Reflection

1. What are the real issues for Jim?

2. Are there other options that he might not have thought of?

3. If you were the literacy coach, what would you advise Jim to do?

Exchange

You have read the "'X-ed' Change" and the chapter. What do you think Barbara sees as the most important things missing in her team experience? What do you think Jessie should suggest to Barbara about the team? What could Barbara say to her literacy coach that wouldn't alienate the coach?

Utilizing Scaffolds to Expand Success

Once a foundation has been laid, we usually see scaffolds raised to support workers in the construction of a building. Just like any construction project, the literacy leadership team has to raise scaffolds to ensure sustaining and expanding success. Of course, just like a building, when completed, the scaffolds are put away until new work needs to be done. By recognizing and utilizing these scaffolds, literacy leadership teams can continue to tackle adaptive challenges to improve learning and instruction. The scaffolds that support the construction of a building are made of metal and wood. The scaffolds that support the work of a literacy leadership team are made with a knowledgeable literacy coach, a long-term schoolwide plan, and district and state support. The literacy leadership team will be better equipped to tackle adaptive challenges with these scaffolds in place

Because literacy coaches' primary responsibility is the professional learning of teacher colleagues, they are in a prime position to serve as a scaffold for a literacy leadership team. Through the literacy coach, the team has a built-in mechanism for providing professional learning opportunities. The team and the literacy coach are a powerful formula to sustain and expand success. Coupled with a long-term schoolwide plan, the literacy leadership team can make great strides in improving learning and instruction. The additional scaffold of district and state support will allow literacy leadership teams to assist not only their school in making forward shifts but also their district and state by highlighting what works with the proper determination and support.

Chapter 10

Utilizing the Literacy Coach

"X-ed" Change

Jack, a fifth-grade teacher, wanted the literacy coach to make some observational visits to his classroom. He thought it would be the best way to see why some students weren't doing as well, even though he believed they were all academically "sound." He approached the coach for help.

Jack: Hi Betty. Thanks for taking time to see me. I have a couple of things that are going on with some of my students and I was wondering if you could make time to come in and observe my teaching and their learning. Some of the students aren't doing as well as I think they should be doing, and I was wondering if it is something in my teaching style that is not working for them.

Betty: Oh, Jack, I would be happy to come in and observe. How does the first of the month sound to you?

Jack: Well, I was really hoping that you could get by a little sooner than that—maybe next week?

Betty: I'll see if I can rearrange my schedule. (She opens her day planner and starts reeling off a list of things.) I have a meeting with my coordinator, then there is a mini-workshop that I have been asked to do, a meeting with the principal, and I have requested a half day off for personal reasons toward the end of this month. Okay, I do have a little time two weeks from today around 11:00.

Jack: I guess that will have to do. I'll see you then.

On the appointed day, Betty shows up with her clipboard and a list of questions she wants Jack to answer about the students. He really wants her to just observe the class to see what is going on. She tells him that he needs to be focused on the one issue he needs addressing because she doesn't have time right now to be more "global." She takes a seat beside his desk and starts in on the questions.

Jack, increasingly more frustrated, just decides to give the students something to do at their seats, and answer her questions. After all the questions had been responded to Betty tells him that she will analyze his answers and get back to him with another time to visit. Jack just thanks her for her time and sees her to the door.

Read the chapter, the libretto, and reflections and think about how this "'X-ed' Change" can be turned into a positive and rewarding experience for Jack.

In *The Literacy Coach: Guiding in the Right Direction* (Puig & Froelich, 2007) we introduced the concept that coaching is professional learning on a continuum of varying support. On that continuum of coaching we proposed supporting study groups and literacy leadership teams as one aspect of literacy coaching or, better said, "part of the job of a literacy coach." Our premise for developing the concept of literacy coaching as a continuum is based on years of personal experiences, the current literature, and serving as literacy coaches at a school site where we coached and were coached by colleagues in a variety of contexts. This led us to conclude that literacy coaching was not just about a preconference, an observation, and a postconference, although we do acknowledge that the preconference, observation, postconference model of literacy coaching is a powerful model to promote forward shifts. Literacy coaching is so much more than just that one model. As we learn more and more about the complex job of a literacy coach, the current literature published on literacy coaching confirms our original proposal that literacy coaching is multifaceted, recursive, and complex (Walpole & McKenna, 2004; Lyons & Pinnell, 2001; Casey, 2006; Toll, 2004; Knight, 2007).

From the beginning of this book, we have proposed that the literacy coach serve as the conduit for professional learning of the literacy leadership team. Can a literacy leadership team exist without a literacy coach? *Yes.* There are actually many. Although literacy coaching is currently in vogue as a model for school reform, many districts and schools have not embraced the concept for a variety of reasons. We have found that literacy leadership teams that do rely on a literacy coach for guidance have a keener focus on adaptive challenges. In those cases, the literacy coach is not viewed as an expert but rather as a lead learner. As we continue to learn and our knowledge of literacy coaching evolves, we have chosen the term *lead learner* rather than *co-learner* because it clearly addresses the behavior that effective and efficient literacy coaches are to model for life-long learning. *When literacy coaches establish themselves as lead learners and approach literacy coaching on a continuum of professional learning, resistance is diminished and collaboration is increased.* Moreover, diminishing resistance and increasing collaboration through ongoing job-embedded professional learning is also a primary focus for literacy leadership teams. Consequently, both literacy coaches and literacy leadership teams have a common ground to develop common goals or adaptive challenges and to ensure that conditions for learning (Cambourne, 1988) are in place and are looked on as necessary for learning and instruction. We encourage literacy leadership teams to adopt and rely on a knowledgeable literacy coach to serve as a lead learner. When a literacy coach is a lead learner, he or she guides a literacy leadership team through the literacy leadership team investigative cycle (Figure 6.1). The literacy leadership team investigative cycle is a system assembled to sustain and expand success.

It is up to the principal, the literacy coach, and the literacy leadership team to ensure that a literacy coach's job is clearly defined if the coach is to serve as a professional learning support for an entire school. In many cases, literacy coaches have surfaced from their participation in a literacy leadership team at the school site. Literacy coaches who evolve from a school literacy leadership team usually have the advantage that they have developed a rapport with the team and other classroom colleagues at their school site over time. Additionally, we have found that when literacy coaches come from a school literacy leadership team, there is less resistance from teacher colleagues to classroom visits and observations.

Once a literacy coach is selected, the question, which is still the question for a plethora of research currently being conducted, is: What does a literacy coach do? *The Literacy Coach: Guiding in the Right Direction* (Puig & Froelich, 2007) provides a sample work week for literacy coaches (see Figure 10.1). At the top of the list (and always controversial), we make the claim that effective and efficient literacy coaches work with students at least 40 percent of their workweek. We argue that when literacy coaches are removed from students, the job of the literacy coach becomes blurred. When this blurring occurs, literacy coaches are assigned to extensive data-entry positions, hall duty, bus duty, cafeteria duty, and the proverbial "other duties as assigned," removing them from the reason that their jobs exist—to directly support students and the teachers.

We also have to clarify that we *do not* intend for this to mean that the literacy coach be the teacher of record. The literacy coach can never be the teacher of record for a given cohort of students. When this occurs, the title and obligations of a literacy coach need to be reconsidered. A literacy coach has to have the scheduling freedom to visit with colleagues and other classrooms if he or she is truly to be coaching.

It cannot be stated clearly enough that principals, literacy coaches, and literacy leadership teams must have a clear understanding of the job requirements of a literacy coach, if the literacy leadership team is going to rely on a literacy coach to guide the team effectively and efficiently. An honest and open discussion based on Figure 10.1 is a critical step for literacy leadership teams that plan on utilizing a literacy coach to guide them as a lead learner. The operative word here is guide. *A literacy coach who serves as a lead learner never dictates a direction, but through research and data (formal and informal) guides the team to recognize and investigate adaptive challenges.* In order for the literacy leadership team to realize the potential of the literacy coach, we will review literacy coaching as a continuum. See Figure 10.2.

FIGURE 10.1
What Does a Literacy Coach Do?

40% of the workweek: learning and instruction with students; may include data collecting (15 hrs/per week)

20% of the workweek: dialogic conversations with teacher and observations (7.5 hrs/per week)

10% of the workweek: providing observation lessons (3.75 hrs/per week)

20% of the workweek: planning and preparing for in-service sessions; data entry and analysis (7.5 hrs/per week)

10% of the workweek: professional book study (3.75 hrs/per week)

Note: Based on an average 37.5-hour teacher contract workweek.

Ongoing Job-Embedded Professional Learning

The literature is clear that the transmission model for professional learning has very little impact on classroom instruction (Joyce & Showers, 2003; Costa & Garmston, 2002). We have read over and over that the best professional learning is ongoing and job embedded. Hence, because of research, we have the current popular belief of the importance of literacy coaching in education to better improve learning and instruction. Yet, what is meant by *ongoing*? What is meant by *job embedded*? It is apparent that the research has been misinterpreted or ignored when so many literacy coaches report investing so little time where instruction takes place—the classroom.

FIGURE 10.2

A Comprehensive Landscape of Support for Professional Learning

Continuum of Coaching

Interactive coaching

Intraactive coaching

← ——————————————————————————————————————→

Facilitate a **workshop or session** to improve learning and instruction	Provide an **observation lesson** to improve learning and instruction	**Co-teach** with a host teacher in an observation classroom to improve learning and instruction	**Confer, observe,** and **debrief** to improve learning and instruction	Facilitate a **study group or literacy leadership team** investigating adaptive challenges to improve learning and instruction	Facilitate **action research** to seek resources after reflection to improve learning and instruction

Increased external scaffolding

Decreased external scaffolding

← ——————————————————————————————————————→

Subject-centered pedagogy

Solution-seeking andragogy

Transformations may occur when the teacher or his or her coaches are provided opportunities to observe, co-teach, confer, study, research, and reflect on practices based on behavioral evidence.

Note: The term *observation lesson* has been used to replace *demonstration lesson* to denote the opportunity being provided versus a model lesson to emulate.

To us, ongoing implies that professional learning for teachers in K–12 never ceases and professional learning opportunities are regularly scheduled and of consistent high quality. We define *regularly scheduled* as at least 90 minutes once every two weeks in order to sustain success, when the plan is to expand success. When serious consideration is given to learning and instruction, this time should be nonnegotiable. High-quality professional learning cannot occur in 15 minutes or during a teacher's planning period.

If professional learning opportunities are scheduled for full days, we encourage you to schedule the day into 90-minute sessions with 15-minute breaks in between as downtime for processing information informally with colleagues or personal reflection. Professional learning opportunities that take place once every two to three months or last less than an hour and a half at a time seem to have the same impact as the mass production in-service meeting. Mass production works when building automobiles, but it does not work when supporting the multidimensional development of human minds—especially when the goal is improving the complex acts of learning and instruction.

Job-embedded professional learning is generally accepted as relevant on-the-job learning. Effective and efficient literacy coaches provide job-embedded learning when they interact with colleagues at a school. True job-embedded learning does not burden literacy coaches, literacy leadership teams, teachers, or students with finding time for learning since learning and instruction are addressed within the context of the school or classroom during contractual school time. Job-embedded learning relies heavily on the Vygotskian concept of assisted performance (Tharp & Gallimore, 1988) and Cazden's (1988) performance before competence. The focus of job-embedded professional learning is on *doing* with assistance rather than just seeing and hearing.

Although ongoing job-embedded learning appears to be a more effective and efficient manner to improve learning and instruction, we do not dismiss the contributions that enthusiastic consultants or attending workshops make to professional learning. The concerns arise when that is the only type of professional learning provided over time, and that these two approaches have no follow up to determine whether they have been successful in their application to the classroom. Attending workshops and hiring consultants is sometimes a necessity to infuse new language for thinking so that we can tackle adaptive challenges.

Because there is limited time, materials, and money, the concept of ongoing job-embedded learning forces literacy coaches and literacy leadership teams to address professional learning, in and of itself, as an adaptive challenge. With professional learning as an adaptive challenge in mind, the literature, as well as personal experiences, beg for literacy coaching to be viewed on a broad-spectrum landscape of support. Furthermore, in order for the literacy leadership team and literacy coach to sustain and expand success, a broad-spectrum landscape of support means that literacy coaching has to be viewed on a continuum fluctuating back and forth from face-to-face interaction to intraaction (personal reflection). One size has never fit all.

Literacy Coaching as a Continuum

The framework for understanding literacy coaching as a continuum opens up a world of possibilities for literacy leadership teams to address adaptive challenges in learning and teaching. Literacy coaching as a continuum is a framework for thinking about the job requirements of the literacy coach and how the literacy coach can support the literacy leadership team in tackling adaptive challenges. Although the continuum of coaching (Figure 10.2) has a limited number of professional learning opportunities, it is certainly not an exhaustive list of supportive activities. Other professional learning opportunities can certainly be added to the continuum of coaching. The big idea is that there is more than one way to coach or support learners and that investing too much time in one given area will be counterproductive over time. Although the continuum addresses literacy coaches specifically, both literacy leadership teams and literacy coaches must continually move back and forth on the continuum if they are to be constantly questioning and growing. Essentially, borrowing from the Maori proverb, you are either "green and growing or ripe and rotting."

Even though the continuum of coaching is illustrated (Figure 10.2) in a very linear fashion, it is not. There is no particular starting point or ending point for learning to begin and finish. One thing is for certain, though—if too much time is invested in one area, you begin to ripen and rot in others. The late Dr. Marie Clay has been described as always stirring the waters (Gaffney & Askew, 1999). When she accepted a lifetime achievement award at the National Reading Conference, she borrowed from the New Zealand poet Allen Curnow the line "Simply by sailing in a different direction you could enlarge the world." Our point is that a literacy leadership team and a literacy coach cannot enlarge their world if they do not sail in a different direction on what we propose as a continuum of coaching.

Facilitating a Workshop

When a literacy coach is charged with introducing a new instructional practice to a group of teachers or when new language needs to be introduced to promote alternative thinking, a workshop may be the venue. Facilitating a workshop is a highly supportive, subject-centered, and interactive endeavor to scaffold professional learning on a continuum of literacy coaching. Effective and efficient literacy coaches facilitate relevant and engaging workshops based on teachers' strengths and needs. Assessment and evaluation will make a workshop relevant while relationships and experiences make it engaging. Workshops facilitated by literacy coaches at the school level should always be based on analyzed formal and informal data. *Vertical and horizontal data have to be cross-checked or co-triangulated for a true adaptive challenge to be identified.*

In schools that have active literacy leadership teams, the literacy coach takes the lead to address an adaptive challenge after working collaboratively with the team. The best decisions for addressing an adaptive challenge are made in collaboration with the team. Once a specific adaptive challenge has been identified and it can be addressed through professional learning, it then becomes the responsibility of the literacy coach to generate a "menu" for professional learning. We use the term *menu* rather than *agenda* since it implies that the responsibility for learning is on the learner. For example, when we go to a restaurant, we are given a menu and the expectation is that we will select what we want to eat based on what we hunger for. When facilitating a workshop for adults, the expectation needs to be in place that the participants are ultimately responsible for their learning and what they select to learn is what they hunger to learn.

Create a template for organizing a 90-minute workshop with colleagues at a school site. The template should be thought of as a menu of materials and activities to engage participants in the professional learning experience. Additionally, the menu has to take into account Cambourne's (1988) conditions *of* learning and utilized as conditions *for* learning. These questions may be a springboard for a rich discussion between the literacy coach and the literacy leadership team in the development of a menu for professional learning:

- How will participants be immersed in the content?
- What kinds of demonstrations are needed based on data?
- What are the expectations during and after the workshop?
- Who is responsible for learning and instruction?
- What kinds of responses will be provided?
- How will approximations be considered?
- What types of experiences are necessary to promote engagement?
- How will the information be employed for future use?

A general outline for facilitating a workshop might include length of time, benefit or benefits for participants as it relates to learning and instruction based on assessment and evaluation, possible materials and activities, a closing activity, and an evaluation to gauge future in-services.

Since most professional learning opportunities are usually provided for teachers at the end of their workday, many literacy coaches provide healthy snacks and refreshments as a gesture of welcome. We all know, of course, that chocolate is always welcome. If working with a literacy leadership team, the literacy leadership team members may rotate the responsibility for providing snacks and refreshments over time so the responsibility does not become an expectation that the literacy coach will always provide the snacks.

As a rule of thumb, when facilitating a workshop, think of yourself as an ethnographer constantly studying and responding to your participants. In ethnographic research, data are triangulated by collecting participant observations, nonparticipant observations, and artifacts (Spradley, 1980; Frank, 1999). As a facilitator, be sure to balance your interactive discussion with personal experiences (participant observations), affirming remarks (based on nonparticipant observations), and use of tangible items to make points. Think of a dynamic presenter or facilitator you have heard recently. Most dynamic presenters make personal stories, make immediate observations from watching or listening to participants, and utilize such artifacts as PowerPoint presentations, books, or handouts. These dynamic facilitators triangulate and balance their presentations to engage participants. To create engaging and memorable presentations, you have to balance the presentations with personal stories, immediate observations, and artifacts. When a presentation is not balanced, participants tend to tune speakers out. Additionally, our top 10 recommendations for facilitating a workshop are:

■ Start with an introduction that will hook your audience by stating the benefits of the workshop to learning and instruction.

■ Present data selectively and succinctly.

■ If you use a visual presentation (e.g., PowerPoint), print should never be smaller than 32 points.

■ When using quotations in a visual presentation, let the audience read it silently first before reading it yourself.

■ Make eye contact with different members of your audience in all locations of the room.

■ Write out your talk, double-spaced, 14-point type, and rehearse it.

■ If you use PowerPoint, learn how to use it first.

■ If time is limited, your introduction and closing are generally the most memorable information; therefore, eliminate from the middle.

■ Do not keep your audience hanging with "one more thing."

■ Closings should have a personal and emotional hook.

Providing an Observation Lesson

Another dimension of a literacy coach's task is providing observation lessons. Observation lessons tend to be a bit subject centered in that a specific instructional practice is employed for a specific reason. It is quite a supportive endeavor in the process of learning and instruction, but not quite as supportive as facilitating a workshop. Here the interaction is a bit more personal than the support provided in a workshop environment. We purposefully are steering clear of the terms *model lesson* and *demonstration lesson* because we have seen so many model lessons that were not. Plus, labeling a lesson as a "model" implies perfection. In actuality, *observation lesson* is a better descriptor of what we are trying to accomplish when working with colleagues. We are providing a professional learning opportunity to observe a lesson. An observation lesson is a time when the literacy coach works with students using a particular instructional practice while a colleague or colleagues observe the lesson. Classroom teachers always appreciate colleagues who provide the opportunity to observe an instructional practice that they are curious about implementing. Think of how many times you have walked away from a workshop and used the phrase, "I need to see it." Providing an observation lesson is the answer to "I need to see it."

Generally, setting up an observation lesson begins with teachers requesting this level of support. At times, however, the literacy coach may request class time from a classroom teacher to provide an observation lesson for the coach's personal professional learning. When the request is made, regardless of who makes it, it is always a good idea to set some ground rules so that it is a productive learning and instructional experience for the classroom teacher, the students, and the literacy coach. Based on our personal experiences in providing observations lessons (in other words, based on the many mistakes we have made along the way), we strongly recommend that the following ground rules be previewed and discussed in advance in order for observation lessons to be powerful professional learning and instructional experiences:

- A specific and respectful time must be scheduled for the observation lesson and the debriefing of the lesson afterwards.

- Prior to the observation lesson, the literacy coach is responsible for visiting the classroom numerous times to know the students and learn their strengths and needs.

- The classroom teacher clearly understands that she or he is to be observing and taking notes that will be used for discussion during the scheduled debriefing.

- The literacy coach has a clear understanding of the research base for the instructional practice demonstrated.

- The literacy coach must have a clear understanding of literacy as a process in order to interact effectively and efficiently with the students during the lesson.

- Some form of documented formal or informal assessment needs to be incorporated into the observation lesson.

- A plan for follow-up where the teacher employs the instructional practice that was demonstrated during the observation lesson needs to be established during the debriefing.

Providing observation lessons can be a two-edge sword for literacy coaches, and literacy leadership teams need to understand that. As we all know, any lesson has the potential to go awry. Yet, when literacy coaches provide observation lessons with the attitude and mentality that this is an opportunity for "learning and instruction," even the worst case scenario can be productive. Our worst lessons have served us as rich experiences to prompt some breakthrough dialogue on what worked and what didn't and why. Furthermore, some of our worst lessons have leveled the playing field with colleagues, presenting us as a lead learner rather than an expert, and have served as a foundation for a long and trusting relationship, which is essential in literacy coaching. We cannot stress enough, though, that to ensure a successful observation lesson, the literacy coach has to know the students and their strengths and needs. Without this working knowledge about the students, observations lessons become another dog and pony show with minimal impact on improving learning and instruction.

Co-Teaching in an Observation Classroom

In a co-teaching situation the host teacher and the guest teacher (in this case, the literacy coach) share the responsibility for learning and instruction with a consistent cohort of students. Ideally, over time the students see the host teacher and the guest teacher as simply their teachers. Co-teaching in an observation classroom is the ideal laboratory for literacy coaches to flourish in their knowledge of literacy learning and instruction. On the continuum of coaching, we place co-teaching in an observation classroom as a hybrid of support where the experience is still interactive but somewhat subject centered and solution seeking simultaneously. Literacy coaches who have adopted co-teaching in an observation classroom as a form of personal professional learning have found it to be a rewarding experience with many benefits. When involved in a co-teaching situation, literacy coaches are not viewed as administrators who are there to "fix" teachers. By placing themselves in a teaching position, literacy coaches will face the realities that classroom teachers face on a daily basis and provide a rich source of experiences to seek solutions *with* colleagues, not *for* colleagues.

Like any relationship, co-teaching in an observation classroom has to be nurtured with the understanding that a primary purpose is for new instructional practices to be employed. Since the literacy coach is responsible for providing professional learning opportunities for other colleagues, host teachers have to accept a literacy coach's need for flexibility in scheduling her or his class time. Although a literacy coach may invest a great deal of time in the same classroom when co-teaching, there will be times when the literacy coach has to provide professional learning opportunities for other colleagues in other classrooms.

In our experiences as literacy coaches and facilitators of courses for literacy coaches, we have found that during the first semester of a school year, more time is invested in co-teaching with less time during the second semester. In some cases, elementary school literacy coaches have co-taught in a primary grade (K–2) during the first semester and then switch to co-teaching in an intermediate grade (3–5) to build up their knowledge of literacy learning and instruction across grade levels. The advantage of this latter model is that elementary schools can have the luxury of a primary and an intermediate observation classroom for teachers to visit. At the middle and high school levels, literacy coaches may co-teach in a reading or language arts classroom during the first semester and proceed to co-teach in a content area (mathematics, science, social studies, etc.) classroom during the second semester for the same reason as their elementary counterparts—to build up their knowledge of literacy learning and instruction across grade levels and, in this case, content areas. As with the elementary counterparts, the advantage of this model is that a reading/language arts and a specific content area observation classroom can be set up for other teachers to visit without ever leaving the campus.

A big advantage to a school when literacy coaches co-teach with a host teacher is that it primes the school as a learning organization (Senge, 1990) and sets the stage for developing observation classrooms where other teachers on campus can visit to reflect, reenergize, and revitalize their own learning and instruction. Of course, setting up an observation classroom requires planning, time, and commitment from the host teacher, the literacy coach, and the literacy leadership team. In setting up an observation classroom where the literacy coach is the co-teacher, the following considerations have to be taken into account by the literacy leadership team:

- A variety of genres and multileveled materials must be present to accommodate the learning needs of the students.

- The furniture and its placement in the room should be conducive for learning.

- The number of students in the host classroom should be the same as in all classrooms.

- Check the availability of technology aids.

- The focus should be on learning and instruction, not on a published sequence of materials, although a published sequence of materials may be incorporated.

- It should be evident that the classroom is driven by ongoing formal and informal assessment.

- Age-appropriate instructional practices need to be visibly in place.

- Set aside some release time for the host teacher to debrief with visiting colleagues.

- An age- and grade-level-appropriate literacy framework is in place that supports and reflects students' growing knowledge from kindergarten through grade 12.

We have found that successful observation classrooms are those that are highly supported by literacy coaches who co-teach in them. Prevalent in observation classrooms is also a clear and succinct literacy framework that takes into account where students are coming from and where they will be going. For example, working with the end in mind, ideally high school (9–12) observation classrooms have a literacy framework that builds on the work started by the middle school colleagues. In turn, a middle school (6–8) observation classroom implements a literacy framework that builds on the work that the elementary school intermediate grade (3–5) colleagues started, and an observation classroom in the intermediate grades builds on the work that the primary (K–2) teachers started. This highly buttressed literacy framework guides the organization of observation classrooms at any grade level and supports students as they evolve through their K–12 academic careers.

Conferring, Observing, and Debriefing

For the conferring, observing, and debriefing level of coaching to take place, a lot of trust has to be established. Without a strong sense of trust, this level of coaching can be counterproductive for improving learning and instruction. Some food for thought when considering the issue of trust is Tschannen-Moran's (2004) five facets of trust: benevolence, honesty, openness, reliability, and competence. Once trust has been established, the literacy coach can proceed to this stage or level of coaching. This level of coaching has the potential to be the most productive to promote forward shifts in learning and instruction. It also has the most potential for back-firing, since it involves an intimate relationship between a teacher and a literacy coach. It has been our experience that this level of coaching is also the one that most literacy coaches have received the least in-service on. Consequently, it is not surprising when the majority of literacy coaches we have had conversations with do not engage in literacy coaching at this level. Nonetheless, it is another level of coaching on a continuum of professional learning experiences to improve learning and instruction.

There are two routes to take when approaching coaching from the con-ferring, observing, debriefing model. Although both routes involve the same processes, the nature of the conversations will be different. One conference may be an introductory conversation with the literacy coach explaining that he or she will be in the classroom as an ethnographer, collecting participant observations, nonparticipant observations, and artifacts to determine a pos-sible coaching point or two based on student behaviors. Saying that the observation will focus on student behavior is critical. *Coaching is not about fix-ing a colleague. It is about improving learning and instruction.*

An alternative conference may involve a dialogic conversation between the teacher and the literacy coach to seek a solution to a concern the teacher may have. Both approaches have their advantages and disadvantages over the other. We encourage literacy coaches and literacy leadership teams to investigate the advantages and disadvantages of one over the other in rela-tion to the teachers at individual schools. With experienced teachers, engag-ing in a dialogic conversation may appear on the surface to be a productive route to take, while at the same time, adopting an ethnographic perspective with novice teachers may seem more appropriate.

This level of coaching on the continuum (Figure 10.2) strikes a balance between interactive and intraactive. It is a sensitive dance between a sub-ject-centered orientation and a solution-seeking orientation, with the focus always on student behavior that is based on students' strengths and needs. Consequently, observing is dependent on the type of conversation that took place prior to the observation. If the decision was made that the coach was entering the classroom from an ethnographic perspective, the observation will evolve as the lesson progresses with one or two coaching points sur-facing for discussion in the debriefing. To the contrary, if the conversation revolved around a request for support and a concern the teacher had, the observation should focus on specific student behavior for solution seeking with the teacher during the debriefing addressing the teacher's concern.

The challenge with always addressing the teacher's concern, is that sometimes other issues that impede learning and instruction will be observed that were unplanned or not discussed in the original conference. For this reason, effective and efficient literacy coaches need to be flexible with which route to take when supporting colleagues at this juncture on the continuum of coaching. Although conferring, observing, and coaching are listed on the continuum of coaching as one form of coaching, there are at least two ways of addressing coaching within this model. The decision to use one model over the other is dependent on the teacher being served.

Facilitating a Study Group or Literacy Leadership Team

Although Chapter 9 in this text addresses developing a study group and this entire book is on literacy leadership teams, we included this section to highlight the fact that facilitating a study group or literacy leadership team is another form of literacy coaching to improve learning and instruction. This section is included here primarily for literacy leadership team members to take note that literacy coaching on a continuum involves many moves to support learning for everyone at a school site. On the continuum of coaching we consider the role of the literacy coach as less supportive when he or she is facilitating a study group or literacy leadership team. The literacy coach in this role is promoting more intraactive behavior of colleagues by encouraging and promoting active solution seeking. At this point on the continuum of coaching, the literacy coach truly does become a lead learner.

In order to facilitate a study group or a literacy leadership team with a focus on learning and instruction, a literacy coach has to take into account that the group or the team needs to:

- Understand literacy learning as a process.
- Establish ground rules for the study group or team meetings.
- Understand the conditions of learning and how they apply to the classroom and school.
- Develop a common language to minimize misinterpretation.
- Identify and honor members and their experiences.
- Learn how to control personal pedagogical passions.
- Address adaptive challenges effectively and efficiently using documented data.

In addition to these points, a critical activity for facilitating a study or literacy leadership team is setting a mutually agreed-on calendar of meetings. Many colleagues of ours will attest that the most productive study groups and literacy leadership teams are the ones that have looked ahead and have literally blocked their calendar with future meeting dates. Setting calendars sends a clear and important message to all members of a study group or literacy leadership team. It confirms the seriousness to commit and communicates to all member that forward shifts take time. Without setting calendars upfront, meetings become haphazard, impeding sustaining and expanding success.

Facilitating Collaborative Action Research

On the opposite end of the continuum of coaching we have placed collaborative action research as another form of literacy coaching that promotes reflection or intraaction. Although the term *action research* was coined around 1944 by Kurt Lewin at MIT and appeared in a 1946 paper titled "Action Research and Minority Problems," it is now a common term in professional learning. Action research is the systematic and recursive, yet contingent, method of questioning, researching, planning, executing, assessing, and reflecting. In essence, the process mirrors what learners do, as we have described in Chapter 4 in a model of literacy as a process (Figure 4.1) and in Chapter 5 as the literacy leadership team investigative cycle (Figure 5.1).

Facilitating and participating in collaborative action research promotes the acquisition of new knowledge, encourages and executes change, and focuses on improving learning and instruction (Stringer, 1996). Research confirms that the reflective nature of the collaborative action research process empowers teachers to improve learning and instruction (Bennett, 1994; Hubbard & Powers, 1999; Glanz, 2003). Kemmis and McTaggert (1988) describe essential components of collaborative action research that include creating an action plan for improving learning and instruction; executing the plan; assessing and documenting change; and reflecting on the change to promote forward shifts. The experience of engaging in collaborative action research encourages forward shifts in instructional practices (Fullan, 2000).

Collaborative action research can be categorized into two approaches: deductive and inductive. The first focuses on executing an action plan, whereas the latter focuses on preparation for an action. The *deductive approach* executes an action plan, tracks implementation issues, and evaluates the final outcomes. The *inductive approach* is to conduct collaborative action research to seek adaptive challenges or to find out what adaptive challenges need to be addressed in a specific learning and instruction situation. Mills (2003) created the following design for facilitating a deductive approach to collaborative action research:

- Identify an adaptive challenge.
- Highlight particular attributes of the adaptive challenge.
- Generate questions to explore.
- Describe the novel practice to be executed.
- Create a schedule for implementation.
- Describe the necessary personnel to be involved in the collaboration.
- List resources to be used or investigated.
- Explain the vertical and horizontal data needed.
- Create a plan for assessment and evaluation of the data.
- Decide on supportive material for investigating.
- Execute the plan to address the adaptive challenge.
- Share outcomes.

Burns (1999) proposes an inductive approach to collaborative action research that utilizes the following interconnected practices:

- Explore an issue in learning and instruction.
- Identify adaptive challenges.
- Assess how the adaptive challenges relate in the context of the research.
- Collaboratively seek solutions to an adaptive challenge.
- Gather vertical and horizontal data to determine an action plan.
- Design an action plan to address the adaptive challenge based on the data collected.

Both inductive and deductive approaches of collaborative action research involve collecting contextualized vertical and horizontal data. A variety of relevant formal and informal assessment is used in both approaches. Commonly used formal and informal assessments are:

- Attendance records
- Standardized tests and scores
- Lesson plans
- Student writing samples
- Writing rubrics
- Running records
- Chapter tests
- End-of-unit tests
- Surveys
- Questionnaire
- Anecdotal notes
- Planbooks
- Report card grades
- Audio and videotapes
- Free and reduced lunch counts

Collaborative action research is relevant and pertinent to specific adaptive challenges for a specific school. It converts tacit understandings of learning and instruction into explicit and documented information that can be shared with district administration and communities. Generally, outcomes from collaborative action research leads to confirmation or rejection of individual interpretations, observations, and instincts based on systematically collected vertical and horizontal data over time. More importantly, when literacy coaches facilitate collaborative action research in their school site, it promotes a collaborative culture of change (Fullan, 2000). Consequently, literacy coaches, literacy leadership teams, and classroom teachers become more resourceful and less dependent on external sources for seeking solutions to learning and instruction that directly impact their school and community (Fullan, 2000).

Summary

The job of a literacy coach is multifaceted and complex, like all learning and instruction. A literacy coach working in collaboration with a literacy leadership team is a powerful combination to bring about positive change in a school. By carefully investigating and putting on the table the specific duties and obligations of the literacy coach, literacy leadership teams will be better equipped to rely on the literacy coach as a rich resource to guide them as they tackle adaptive challenges.

When a literacy leadership team thinks of literacy coaching on a continuum of professional learning opportunities, it opens the school to a safe culture of learning. It is in this safe culture of learning that principals, literacy coaches, teachers, literacy leadership team members, and students will grow. In this chapter we presented coaching as a continuum that includes facilitating a workshop; providing observation lessons; co-teaching in an observation classroom; conferring, observing, and debriefing; facilitating a study group; and facilitating collaborative action research. We purposefully used verbs to describe the variety of activities that coaches deal with to make that point that effective and efficient literacy coaching is about taking action to improve learning and instruction.

Each activity on the continuum of coaching was given a section to flesh out points for discussion and helpful hints to assist literacy leadership teams in understanding literacy coaching in a broader and more productive sense to support sustaining and expanding success at your school.

Rachel never saw it coming. Right out of the blue, two of her colleagues and mentors told her that they didn't want her to observe or co-teach in their classrooms. These were the two teachers that had taken her under their wings last year when she was a novice teacher. They had really been so helpful to her. What had happened to change all of that?

The previous week Rachel had sent around a schedule to all the seventh-grade teachers to let them know that she was going to be spending some "quality" time with them in their classrooms. She had the times and class schedules for each teacher and expected them to happily respond to her request. Although she was only in her second year of teaching, and she hadn't actually sought out this position of literacy coach, she really wanted the job and thought she could be quite effective. She had read all of the materials her coordinator had provided, she had attended the institute to learn about how to observe and take appropriate notes. She had prepared the schedule just as she had been instructed to do by her assistant principal. She had even remembered to leave off the asterisks that marked the teachers that the principal really wanted to be observed. So what had she missed?

Reflections

1. What was the first thing that Rachel did that she shouldn't have done?

2. What are the overarching issues with Rachel being the literacy coach in this school?

3. How might the coordinator have eliminated this problem before it was created?

4. What would you have said if you had been the mentor teacher to help Rachel understand your position?

Exchange

You have read the "'X-ed' Change" as well as the chapter and the libretto. What issues come to mind that the two literacy coaches have missed? As the literacy coach what would you have done differently? What points were made in the chapter that helped you see clearly how Betty and Rachel should have approached their roles as coach and team leader and turned this scenario from one that would not sustain, or even begin the change cycle, to one that would?

Chapter 11

Developing a Schoolwide Plan

"X-ed" Change

Dr. Danford is the newly hired principal for the largest high school in his district. He is a veteran teacher with 20 years of experience, so he knows the ropes. He plans on using his vast experience to change the culture and the climate at the high school. When he was hired, the superintendent told him that his mandate was to raise test scores, improve the graduation rate, and to make sure that the teachers engaged in ongoing professional learning opportunities. Dr. Danford's plan was to bring all of this up at the first faculty meeting and to introduce the new literacy coach, Vivian Alvarez, who would be providing the in-service as well as building a literacy leadership team. He planned to give teachers who volunteered for the team an extra planning period so that they had plenty of time to work on his agenda.

Dr. Danford began, "Welcome everyone, to our first faculty meeting of the school year. For those of you who haven't gotten around to meeting me, I'm Charles Danford, and I want you to know that I am looking forward to a strong and productive year working with all of you. I know our challenges are many: We have high dropout rates, our scores aren't what they should be, and, without pointing any fingers, I know that several of you haven't kept up with your in-service hours and preparation. Well, things are going to change around here. The superintendent has asked me to make sure that we get up to speed on the new literacy standards. One of the things that we are going to implement is a literacy leadership team, chaired by Mrs. Alvarez, the literacy coach who has been assigned to our school this year.

"Mrs. Alvarez will be selecting a literacy team and, as an added incentive, I am prepared to give each teacher who volunteers for the team an additional planning period. Now don't you all just jump up and rush Mrs. Alvarez. We have a plan in place for the selection process. We are passing around a form that you will fill out and return to her. On this form, please list all the extracurricular activities you are already engaged in. Also please put any outside obligations that would interfere with meeting on a weekly basis. And coaches, I guess that your schedules are like mine—so busy that there is no way you could participate—but if you have a little extra time, and would like to, please feel free to fill out the form. All forms should be turned in no later than Wednesday of next week so we can get this ball rolling as soon as possible. Now, Mrs. Alvarez, do you have a few words you would like to add?"

Mrs. Alvarez, speechless as to what has just occurred, could only shake her head "no" and sit in stunned disbelief that this school year and all her plans for building a complete community of learners was starting off so badly.

After reading the chapter, read the libretto and reflections. Talk with colleagues to find ways that would turn the "'X-ed' Change" into an "Exchange" that would work for the team and the faculty as a whole.

An initial and key endeavor for a literacy leadership team is to develop a long-term schoolwide plan to ensure sustaining and expanding success (Fullan, Hill, & Crevola, 2006). We debated where to place this chapter and realized that without all the previous discussions—such as understanding adult learning, understanding conditions of learning, developing a common language, understanding literacy as a process, and utilizing the literacy coach—attempting to create a long-term plan may be misleading. Consequently, after carefully reading this book and working in collaboration with the literacy coach and a variety of colleagues at a school site, literacy leadership team members can lay out a proposed flexible plan that allows for change and forward shifts in learning and instruction. Without this long-term planning, schools that are interested in sustaining and expanding success will fall prey to instruction *à la mode*. Without a long-term plan, the school will more than likely switch from one instructional program to another without giving any one particular program a chance to evolve. As we have stated earlier, we use the term *program* to indicate a series of instructional practices that support learning and instruction that may or may not include a published series of materials presented in a particular sequence for instruction.

We recommend that prior to long-term planning, this book be read and thoroughly discussed in its entirety to better develop a sense of where the team is coming from and where they want to go. Once this reading and talking has taken place, the team may want to place five blank pieces of chart paper around a room with each one titled "Stage 1," "Stage 2," "Stage 3," "Stage 4," and "Stage 5." With the charts labeled, the team now starts to consider options for the school by developing a multistage implementation plan to support forward shifts in learning and instruction based on vertical and horizontal assessments, all the while keeping in mind the recursive nature of all learning. We purposefully stayed away from labeling the charts "year 1," "year 2," and so on, since no two schools are exactly the same. In some cases, some schools may decide to combine a stage or two depending on what has been set in motion in the past.

We propose a specific five-stage implementation plan for professional learning to sustain and expand success over time (see Figure 11.1). Used in conjunction with the annotated bibliography at the end of this book (Appendix D), the five-stage plan will serve a school well to ensure forward shifts in learning and instruction. It is up to the literacy leadership team to consider our recommendations in combination with the school's strengths and needs. For example, with the school of a highly engaged and well-informed literacy principal, the team may decide to blend Stages 1 and 2 and move forward. Consideration also needs to be given to the fact that the stages can be recursive due to personnel changes and student mobility at a school.

Looking Ahead: Developing and Using a Five-Stage Plan

Stage 1: Development of the Literacy Principal

The first stage in our five-stage plan for sustaining and expanding success is the *development of the literacy principal.* A supportive and knowledgeable literacy principal is a primary catalyst for schools to make forward shifts in learning and instruction (Lambert, 2003; Booth & Roswell, 2007; Puig & Froelich, 2007). The literature is clear that for forward shifts to occur in learning and instruction, the principal has to be an instructional leader first (Lambert, 2003; Lyons & Pinnell, 2001; Booth & Rowsell, 2007). In order for principals to become knowledgeable literacy principals, their professional learning needs to take place over an extended period of time. The best professional learning opportunities we have encountered have always taken place over time. When professional learning occurs over time, participants are given the opportunities to process information and experiment with implementing and refining new practices to support learning and instruction (Fullan, Hill, & Crevola, 2006).

We certainly realize that a principal's time is always tight and there are never enough hours in the day. Nonetheless, if forward shifts in learning and instruction are to be accomplished, time has to be allocated

FIGURE 11.1

Five-Stage Plan for Sustaining and Expanding Success

Stage 1: Development of the Literacy Principal	Five full-day (30 hrs.) professional learning sessions that include classroom briefings, observations, and debriefings ■ Day 1: Literacy as a process and instructional practice ■ Day 2: Using assessment to guide instruction ■ Day 3: Coaching as a continuum of professional learning ■ Day 4: Transformational vs. interactive professional learning ■ Day 5: Organizing for instruction Recommended professional text: *(see Annotated Bibliography, Appendix D)*
Stage 2: Development of Literacy Leadership Team	5 full-day (30 hrs.) professional learning sessions ■ Day 1: Reading as a process and assessment ■ Day 2: Writing as a process and assessment ■ Day 3: Literacy as a process across content areas ■ Day 4: Teaching for reciprocity across content areas ■ Day 5: Creating a professional learning plan that includes a literacy coach Recommended professional text: *(see Annotated Bibliography, Appendix D)*
Stage 3: Job-Embedded Professional Learning of the Literacy Coach	■ 15 graduate-level credits/year-long, or 300 professional development hrs./year-long ■ Case study on high-, average-, and low-progress students ■ Videotape lessons with written reflections ■ *Scaffold study groups* at school level on literacy acquisition and development ■ Teach students on a daily basis ■ Participate in a summer literacy institute ■ Develop course for on-site professional learning in collaboration with the literacy leadership team based on vertical and horizontal assessment Recommended professional text: *(see Annotated Bibliography, Appendix D)*
Stage 4: Job-Embedded Professional Learning of Teachers	■ 40 hrs. on-site professional learning opportunity provided by literacy coach ■ Literacy coach continues to teach students on a daily basis ■ Literacy leadership team continues to reflect on data ■ 36 hrs. ongoing professional learning for literacy coach ■ Ongoing collaboration with literacy coach and literacy leadership team Recommended professional text: *(see Annotated Bibliography, Appendix D)*
Stage 5: Collaborative Action Research	■ 20 hrs. professional learning opportunity provided by literacy coach ■ Literacy coach continues to teach students on a daily basis ■ Literacy leadership team conducts schoolwide action research supported by literacy coach ■ 36 hrs. ongoing professional learning for literacy coach Recommended professional texts: *(see Annotated Bibliography, Appendix D)*

for professional learning. Without professional learning time set aside, school administrators become business managers rather than instructional leaders. Managing the business side of school is a critical and important aspect of the principal's job, but so is the quality of instruction taking place in a school. It does not need to be a dichotomy. We acknowledge that the principal's job is a balancing act and a sensitive dance between administration and instruction. With the support of an effective literacy coach and an efficient literacy leadership team, principals can become part of a learning community and still manage the business of school.

For learning and change to take place, we recommend that in considering a five-stage plan of implementation, the first stage should include approximately 30 hours of professional learning opportunities set aside for principals over an academic school year. These 30 hours should expose principals to understanding literacy as a process, using assessment to guide instruction, understanding coaching on a continuum of professional learning (Puig & Froelich, 2007), developing a clear understanding that learning needs to be transformational (Fullan, Hill, & Crevola, 2006), and what needs to be done to organize for instruction. The 30 hours of professional learning may be five full days of in-service provided for a cadre of principals by a school district or university. An alternative plan may be 30 hours set aside by a cohort of principals to engage in a book study with other principal colleagues. The annotated bibliography (Appendix D) at the end of this book provides some professional texts that we have found to be informative to support principals in becoming effective literacy leaders.

Stage 2: Development of the Literacy Leadership Team

The second stage of an implementation plan that focuses on sustaining and expanding success is the *development of the literacy leadership team.* Chapter 5 in this text supports literacy leadership teams in getting started. Once the team has organized itself, the focus then becomes developing the team for effectiveness and efficiency. For this to occur, the team has to invest time in its own professional learning by engaging in a planned course of study that focuses on understanding literacy acquisition, literacy development, literacy assessment, and literacy instruction (Lent, 2007). Literacy instruction in this instance means across-content areas regardless of the grade level. Additionally, studying and understanding the role of the literacy coach in relation to the team and school is vital. *The literacy coach should be the conduit for professional learning for the literacy leadership team and the principal.*

In order to serve as a conduit for professional learning, the literacy coach has to be viewed as a knowledgeable colleague and a lead learner. Similar to the 30-hour course we recommend for principals, the literacy leadership team may engage and invest their time in 30 hours of professional learning provided by a school district or university. An option to a specific course of study provided by a district or university may be a 30-hour book study involving all members of the literacy leadership team over the span of an academic school year. Summer institutes to support and develop literacy leadership teams can also be taken into account as part of a 30-hour course or plan. In our work with literacy leadership teams, we have found that investing less than 30 hours of professional learning was never sufficient to sustain and expand success at a school.

Stage 3: Job-Embedded Professional Learning of the Literacy Coach

Equipped with a knowledgeable instructional leader and literacy leadership team, the school is ready to move into what we consider Stage 3 of a long-term implementation plan for sustaining and expanding success. In the third stage, the focus is on the *development of the literacy coach*. The development of the literacy coach has to be far more intensive than a literacy principal or a literacy leadership team if he or she is to be the conduit for high-quality professional learning to occur.

For literacy coaches to become effective and efficient lead-learners, we strongly recommend that they participate in a 300-hour course designed and provided either by their districts or a university over one academic year with a focus on literacy development and coaching. Such courses have to include time for literacy coaches to teach students, observe teachers teaching students, and observe literacy coaching. We continue to insist that it is through teaching students on a regular basis that literacy coaches maintain credibility with colleagues (Casey, 2006; Puig & Froelich, 2007). Consequently, any long-term course for literacy coaches has to have time built into it for literacy coaches to teach students. We argue that there is no other way for literacy coaches to hone their learning and instruction so that they can support other colleagues and the literacy leadership team. Since the majority of members on a literacy leadership team are classroom teachers, it is fundamental that the literacy coach have the shared experience of teaching students in order to serve the team and the school as a lead-learner.

Throughout the literacy coach's academic in-service year, her or his responsibilities are to facilitate a professional text-centered *scaffold study group* with colleagues, teach students on a daily basis, work closely with the literacy leadership team, participate as a presenter in a summer literacy institute, and create a year-long course syllabus in collaboration with the literacy leadership team for classroom teachers at their school. The course syllabus needs to specifically state:

- Goal and purpose
- Objectives
- Resources
- Assignments
- Evaluation
- Timetable
- Rationale
- Number of hours
- Equipment and facilities
- Target audience
- Information on the facilitator

This variety of learning experiences will provide the literacy coach the necessary background to tackle adaptive challenges proactively. An ideal day of in-service for literacy coaches will look like the following agenda:

8:00–8:30	Observation briefing by literacy coach at the host school
8:30–10:00	Classroom observation
10:00–10:15	Break/downtime for processing information
10:15–11:15	Observation debriefing and categorizing coaching points
11:15–12:30	Lunch/downtime for processing information
12:30–1:45	Viewing two videotaped lessons conducted by peer coaches
1:45–2:00	Break/downtime for processing information
2:00–3:00	Professional book talk (taking theory to practice)

Figure 11.2 illustrates a proposed year-long course that districts or universities may use to flesh out a vigorous and relevant course for literacy coaches.

Stage 4: Job-Embedded Professional Learning of Teachers

In the next stage of development, the literacy coach provides a 40-hour year-long on-site professional learning opportunity to *support classroom teachers* in tackling adaptive challenges in their classrooms. This 40-hour course is constructed in collaboration with the literacy leadership team to ensure sustaining and expanding success. It is best to ground the course by using a specific professional text that focuses on instructional practices grounded in theory and supported by research. The in-service sessions should be approximately 90 minutes long and be provided every other week. We have found that in-service sessions that last less than 90 minutes never delve deep enough to sustain or expand success. When in-service sessions go beyond the 90 minutes, interim and engaging activities have to be incorporated to maintain a high level of interest. Figure 11.3 delineates a possible 40-hour course for literacy coaches to implement. Initially, the main purpose of the course is to develop a common language and investigate novel instructional practices that promote forward shifts in learning and instruction.

FIGURE 11.2

Year-Long In-Service for Literacy Coaches

August

- Assessment training.
- Oversee administration of baseline data collection; collect baseline data in designated grade levels.
- Attend autumn classes, 7:30 A.M. to 3:00 P.M.
- Reading assignment:

September

- Begin implementation of a literacy lesson framework.
- Meet with peers for *scaffold study group.*
  - Discuss assignment.
  - Send a brief summary of discussion, including new questions that evolved, to the facilitator.
- Attend autumn classes, 7:30 A.M. to 3:00 P.M.
- Reading assignment:

October

- Attend autumn classes, 7:30 A.M. to 3:00 P.M.
- School literacy team building session #1 (tentative).[1]
- Complete baseline data collection.
- Work daily with target group.
  - Implement a literacy lesson framework.
  - Videotape group lesson/guiding readers.
    - Reflect on lesson.[2]
- Meet with peers in scaffold study group.
- Discuss assignment.
- Send a brief summary of discussion, including new questions that evolved, to the facilitator.
- Reading assignment:

November

- Attend autumn classes.
- Work daily with target group.
  - Implement a literacy lesson framework.
  - Videotape group lesson/interactive or shared writing.
    - Reflect on lesson.
- Meet with peers in scaffold study group.
  - Discuss assignment.
  - Send a brief summary of discussion, including new questions that evolved, to the facilitator.
- School literacy team building session #2 (tentative).
- Reading assignment:

December

- Attend autumn classes.
- Work daily with target group.
  - Implement a literacy lesson framework.
  - Videotape group lesson/shared reading.
    - Reflect on lesson.
- Meet with peers in scaffold study group.
  - Discuss assignment.
  - Send a brief summary of discussion, including new questions that evolved, to the trainer.
- School literacy team building session #3 (tentative).
- Reading assignment:

January

- Attend winter classes.
- Work daily with target group.
  - Implement a literacy lesson framework.
  - Videotape group lesson/guided reading.
  - Reflect on lesson.
- Meet with peers in scaffold study group.
  - Discuss assignment.
    - Send a brief summary of discussion, including new questions that evolved, to the facilitator.
- School literacy team building session # 4 (tentative).
- Reading assignment:

February

- Attend winter classes.
- Work daily with target group.
  - Implement the literacy lesson framework.
  - Videotape group lesson/interactive or shared writing.
    - Reflect on lesson.
- Meet with peers in scaffold study group.
  - Discuss assignment.
  - Send a brief summary of discussion, including new questions that evolved, to the trainer.
- Attend professional conference (optional in lieu of classes).
  - Includes preconference session.
- Reading assignment:

March

- Attend winter classes.
- Work daily with target group.
  - Implement a literacy lesson framework.
  - Videotape group lesson/shared reading.
    - Reflect on lesson.
- Meet with peers in scaffold study group.
  - Discuss assignment.
  - Send a brief summary of discussion, including new questions that evolved, to the facilitator.
- School literacy team building session #5 (tentative).
- Reading assignment:
- Prepare for spring testing.

April

- Attend spring classes.
- Work daily with target group.
  - Implement a literacy lesson framework.
  - Videotape session/coaching.
    - Reflect on session.
- Meet with peers in a scaffold study group.
  - Discuss assignment.
  - Send a brief summary of discussion, including new questions that evolved, to the facilitator.
- Reading assignment:

May

- Attend spring classes.
- Work daily with target group.
  - Implement a literacy lesson framework.
  - Videotape session/coaching.
    - Reflect on session.
- Meet with peers in scaffold study group.
  - Send a brief summary of discussion, including new questions that evolved, to the facilitator.

June

- Case studies of the literacy learning of three students summary paper (6–10 pages).
  - Due first week in June.
- Professional reading and reflections.
  - Due second week in June.
    - Full-page summary per chapter.
- Attend classes for 2 weeks at a university site.
- Literacy coaches-in-training will be presenting in a 4-day K–12 literacy institute. Debriefing and graduation ceremony will follow.

[1]**School literacy leadership team building sessions**: A team, comprised of approximately six or more representatives, including the principal, the literacy coach, and faculty, who represent the range of grade levels and programs offered in the school, meet for five full-day seminars. The goal of the team is to develop a school plan for implementing and supporting literacy learning and instruction in their school over the next several years.

[2]**Videotape reflections**: Literacy coaches-in-training are required to send videotapes of their teaching to the facilitator. Each tape must be accompanied by a one-page (double-spaced) analysis of the learning and instruction, supported with quotes from the readings that occurred within the sessions.

Note: (Optional university credit) Nondegree-seeking course credit or certificate will be given upon successful completion of the year-long in-service course. Literacy coaches-in-training may register for a maximum of fifteen (15) credit hours/300 hours.

FIGURE 11.3

Year-Long Course for Classroom Teachers

August	Session 1	Assessment administration
	Session 2	Data analysis and instruction
September	Session 3	Organizing the classroom for instruction
	Session 4	Creating an information-intensive environment
October	Session 5	Precise and intentional instruction
	Session 6	Guiding literacy learners: small-group instruction
November	Session 7	Critical writing instruction
	Session 8	Critical reading instruction
December	Session 9	Working systems of literacy
	Session 10	Assembling working systems
January	Session 11	Teaching for reciprocity
	Session 12	Investigating reading genres
February	Session 13	Investigating writing genres
	Session 14	Interactive spelling instruction
March	Session 15	Interactive phonics instruction
	Session 16	Vocabulary development and instruction
April	Session 17	Teaching for fluency
	Session 18	Teaching for comprehension
May	Session 19	Revisiting the core literacy program
	Session 20	End-of-year data analysis

Stage 5: Collaborative Action Research

While facilitating the 40 hours in-service with classroom teachers, the literacy coach simultaneously is involved in a minimum of 36 hours of continual personal professional learning provided by the district or university to refine his or her coaching. This continual professional learning keeps the literacy coach fresh with research, theory, and instructional practices to constantly be updating learning and instruction.

Summary

No one will dismiss the importance of planning and organizing. For a literacy leadership team to sustain and expand success, it is critical that the literacy leadership team review where they are coming from, where they are, and where they want to go. To accomplish such a goal, the team needs to take into account all stakeholders and compose and construct a contingent five-stage plan that will serve everyone at school.

Based on years of experience, we outlined a variety of professional learning experiences that we have implemented and refined over time to sustain and expand success. The five-stage plan that we proposed in this chapter can be followed exactly as written or adjusted based on your school's strengths and adaptive challenges that need to be tackled. The five-stage plan, sample 40 hours in-service course for teacher colleagues, 30 hours of scaffold study group, and course syllabus recommendations are designed to support and encourage a literacy leadership team to prepare for change over time to sustain and expand success. Implementing a literacy leadership team and utilizing a literacy coach to support the team as a school reform model require long-term planning to improve learning and instruction.

In the next chapter, we have asked Evan B. Lefsky, executive director, *Just Read, Florida!* to share his recommendations based on his experiences at the state level to support the development of literacy leadership teams. The chapter will guide literacy leadership team members in promoting within your district and state to consider developing a K–12 literacy plan, utilizing the literacy coach, and providing a variety of professional learning experiences that states and districts need to consider to ensure forward shifts in learning and instruction.

In our experience as literacy leadership team members and with literacy leadership teams, including Chapter 12 is a gift. The information it contains is critical knowledge for literacy leadership team members in order to promote a schoolwide, districtwide, and statewide network of support, particularly in districts and states with high mobility rates. We know firsthand that a literacy leadership team can exist without the support of the district and state. We also know that recruiting the support of the district and state will amplify a literacy leadership team's mission and accelerate a literacy leadership team in sustaining and expanding success.

LIBRETTO

Patrice was a little nervous about her new position as literacy coach because she was being assigned to a school that she had heard really horrible things about—not your standard poor performance issues, or student discipline issues, but a principal who "ruled" and teachers who couldn't care less about whether the test scores improved. If this were truly the case, they would probably also not be very responsive to becoming members of a literacy leadership team and they certainly wouldn't be interested in allowing a coach into their classrooms no matter what the reason. Patrice made an appointment to meet with the principal to see what she was up against. If the principal "wasn't on board," then it was really going to be an uphill battle all year.

Mr. Billings: Good morning, Patrice. Can I call you Patrice?

Patrice: Absolutely, Mr. Billings.

Mr. Billings: Well, it's good to finally meet you. I have been thinking a lot about what we need to do this year to achieve all the goals the superintendent has for us, as well as the ones I know you have for your new leadership team. Let me tell you what I think you should do first. I think you should survey the faculty to get those teachers who are really interested in joining your team. I have identified several from the choices they made last year when planning their types of conferences or in-service meetings. I think it is important to choose teachers that all "like" you in terms of understanding what literacy really is. I don't see any point in having a team of people who aren't thinking alike. And it's not productive if during every meeting you have to fight people to understand what you are talking about.

Patrice: Mr. Billings, I think the team should be made up of teachers from all the disciplines. What happens if one of those is not on your list?

Mr. Billings: I can assure you, Patrice, some of the content areas are definitely missing from this list, but that's okay. Trust me; you will be better off without them.

Patrice, not knowing what to say, just nodded her head, fearing the worst for this school year.

Reflections

1. What are the central issues in this libretto that the literacy coach must face and find a way to correct?

2. What does Mr. Billings need to know to be better informed about a literacy leadership team?

3. What kinds of materials could Patrice provide Mr. Billings that would help him understand what she needs to be successful in her role as coach and co-learner?

Exchanges

After reading the chapter, the libretto, and reflections, what would you do to turn the "'X-ed' Change" scenario into one in which the coach and the principal are speaking the same language, and have a common goal in mind for the literacy leadership team as well as a long-term plan to tackle adaptive challenges of the school?

Chapter 12

Building State and District Support for Literacy Leadership Teams

Evan B. Lefsky

As states and school districts begin to think about steps necessary to facilitate long-term growth in literacy outcomes for students, the role of school-level leadership, both among principals and distributed leaders, must be at the forefront. As the role of the school-based leader becomes increasingly diverse, the knowledge base of principals must also become increasingly diverse, especially regarding the subject of students with reading and literacy difficulties. Although one school-based administrator cannot possibly know all that it is necessary to know in the area of literacy assessment and instruction, a well-planned and well-developed literacy leadership team can. Therefore, state and local leadership must establish a plan for creating and sustaining school-level literacy leadership teams.

Because of its diverse membership, the literacy leadership team serves as a strong model for infusing an emphasis on literacy across the curriculum. This is a necessary step in any long-range effort to improve literacy outcomes for students. States and local districts must come to the realization that many students who start behind their peers in the area of literacy will need teachers each day who understand how to meet students' unique literacy needs. Only when all teachers understand the important role that they play in students' literacy development will we be able to reach our common goals. The literacy leadership team helps to facilitate this understanding for teachers. It is important for state and district leadership to understand that the emphasis on teacher leadership is not about teachers being involved in the day-to-day administrative duties, but rather "playing to the strength of their classroom expertise" (Scherer, p. 7).

The benefits to states and local districts are important to recognize. This school-level team approach can assist states and local school districts by providing the infrastructure and instructional supports needed to improve teacher retention. The supportive and collaborative environment provided by literacy leadership teams serves as an effective mentoring system for new teachers.

Additionally, utilizing literacy leadership teams is an effective reform model because they contain many of the elements found in the research literature (Deschler, Schumaker, & Woodruff, 2004) that contribute to successful literacy outcomes:

- Literacy improvement is a top priority as reflected by dedication of resources.

- All teachers display a sense of responsibility for improving the literacy outcomes of all students.

- A focus on literacy instruction helps to coordinate instruction across grades, classes, and teachers.

- All instructional practices and programs are validated in the research and matched to student need.

Based on my experiences with a statewide literacy initiative, this chapter details how states can create a coordinated literacy initiative with a focus on building leadership capacity through the establishment of K–12 literacy plans at the district level and literacy leadership teams at the school level.

Establishing Support at the State Level

By establishing reading as a core value, states can create a comprehensive and coordinated K–12 literacy initiative designed to have every child reading at or above grade level and make every citizen a literacy advocate. With these goals in mind, states can provide professional learning opportunities, resources, and support through a variety of statewide projects in order to ensure improved literacy outcomes for all students. Such initiatives can be recognized by the unique, systemic focus they provide for all educators and students. Although many states are just beginning to explicitly extend their K–3 reading focus to the upper grades, a few states have been doing so for several years. These states have already seen substantial results from this investment in a comprehensive K–12 literacy plan to provide research-based reading and writing instruction throughout the curriculum, beginning in the early grades and continuing through high school. The focus of any state- or district-level program should be to create and implement a comprehensive and coordinated literacy model aimed at helping every student become a successful and independent reader.

comprehensive and coordinated literacy model aimed at helping every student become a successful and independent reader.

comprehensive and coordinated literacy model aimed at helping every student become a successful and independent reader.

comprehensive and coordinated literacy model aimed at helping every student become a successful and independent reader.

comprehensive and coordinated literacy model aimed at helping every student become a successful and independent reader.

The K–12 Literacy Plan

The support of the state legislature in ensuring that an annual allocation for literacy instruction is provided through an education finance program is critical to state and local efforts. If recommended and well supported by governors and state boards of education, this action by the state legislature can make literacy a permanent priority and ensure that this priority is funded annually as a part of the public school funding formula. This annual allocation provided by the legislature ensures that there is funding to provide for:

- Highly effective literacy coaches in schools
- Highly effective reading teacher positions in schools
- Literacy leadership team activities
- Infusion of research-based literacy instruction in all content areas
- Continuous, embedded professional learning opportunities and school-based supports and resources to integrate text comprehension strategic activities and writing instruction across the curriculum for all teachers and administrators
- Summer reading camps for students who struggle with literacy
- Before- and after-school literacy program activities
- Diverse instructional resources that are grounded in a strong research base and evidence base
- Distribution of resources based on individual school needs according to students' and teachers' levels of need determined by data
- Intensive interventions for students reading below grade level
- Improvement plans for schools that are not making academic improvements, as determined by student performance data

Once annual literacy funding is established, it is critical that, in order for districts to receive their share of state reading funding, they write a K–12 *comprehensive literacy plan* based on guidance provided by a state literacy initiative stocked with knowledgeable personnel. This plan will be the major tool for coordinating continuous literacy improvement statewide. It provides a focused initiative that guides the work of school-level literacy leadership teams through a uniform yet flexible plan that can be tailored to the needs of individual schools based on the literacy needs of students. The plan holds school districts responsible for guiding and supporting school-level literacy initiatives by focusing on support starting with the superintendent. District-level literacy leadership teams serve as an effective model and stable support system for school-level teams. Once established, close coordination with district- and school-level leadership teams allows states to offer support for high-quality school-level implementation of the plan. This mix of top-down guidance and support with bottom-up initiatives provides the coordination needed for successful literacy reform (Fullan, 1994).

State-Funded University-Based Support

Differentiated support can be offered through university-based area coordinators who work as site-based facilitators of professional learning. These coordinators can work with literacy leadership teams at schools throughout the state based on need and request. They may work with literacy leadership teams as a whole, but they can also provide direct support to literacy coaches and teachers in classrooms. This network of coordinators offers schools high-quality professional learning opportunities that provide educators with rigorous, research-based curriculum and opportunities to practice specific literacy instruction skills in a supported professional environment. In addition to the K–12 literacy plan and university-based area coordinators who support schools, states, and districts wishing to support the work of literacy leadership teams can offer numerous professional learning resources and opportunities during the summer and throughout the school year.

Implementing a K–12 Literacy Leadership Conference

Each summer, states can generate excitement with principals, assistant principals, literacy coaches, and district administrators by implementing a K–12 literacy leadership conference in order to share what works for improving literacy in schools through a multitude of breakout sessions. At this conference, school- and district-level leadership teams share effective practices and learn from their colleagues who have similar challenges through networking opportunities provided throughout the conference. Specific professional learning is geared toward principals and literacy coaches working in collaboration to establish and maintain literacy leadership teams. The knowledge gained at this conference can be directly applied back at the school site with the full literacy leadership team. This provides an opportunity for coaches to work side by side with their school administrators as they learn from effective principal and coach teams, while planning for their own individualized school-level reforms. When coaches and principals jointly partake in this professional learning off campus, they are more likely to engage in professional learning and collaborative efforts toward literacy improvement back on campus with the full literacy leadership team.

K–12 Literacy Coach Academies

One critical element to the success of literacy leadership teams is the participation and leadership of the literacy coach. Regional professional learning opportunities should be provided for elementary and secondary literacy coaches year round so that they may utilize effective coaching skills while working with teachers and students to build literacy skills. These professional learning opportunities should go beyond the classroom coaching role and help to engage coaches in the leadership aspects of their positions that were formerly encompassed by the school or district reading specialist. It is important that states and districts develop rigorous standards for literacy coaches; literacy coaching endorsements and strong professional learning support will provide coaches with the knowledge, resources, and credibility to support the work of literacy leadership teams.

Summer Literacy Leadership Team Institutes

Although states may require that literacy leadership teams be a part of every district's K–12 literacy plan, many schools struggle to establish these teams for a variety of reasons. In some cases, principals do not see the value, viewing it as just one more state mandate, while others do not know where to begin the process. The goal of the summer literacy leadership team institutes is to offer support to school teams wishing to engage in professional learning and literacy planning for the school year. During two-day summer institutes, members of the literacy leadership team create an action plan in order to provide effective literacy instruction for students utilizing the most effective practices and materials. As they do this, they establish a culture of learning and collaboration within the school that spreads to every classroom. This summer professional learning also provides an excellent opportunity for the state-funded university-based area coordinators to work directly with the schools and literacy leadership teams they will support during the school year. These institutes provide the knowledge base and motivation necessary to electrify team members who can actively produce forward shifts at the school level.

Professional Learning Resources

Another method by which states and districts can contribute to the success of literacy leadership teams throughout the school year is by providing strong literacy professional learning opportunities that will act to support a common knowledge base among team members.

States and districts can provide this support through a variety of resources for reading teachers, principals, and content area teachers. A course can be created to support content area reading professional learning intended to provide these teachers with intensive, high-quality professional learning in literacy so they better understand how to assist all students in meeting the literacy demands of their individual content area. Content area teachers who provide reading intervention to low-progress students in lieu of a reading specialist help to build capacity at the school level, allowing students with greater intervention needs to be served with more intensity. These initiatives also help content teachers internalize their role as part of the solution toward improving the literacy abilities of students. *When content teachers are able to have more direct involvement with literacy improvement efforts, they can more readily contribute to the literacy leadership team and schoolwide reform efforts.*

Another initiative states can provide is an on-line literacy learning network. This website for principals, literacy coaches, and classroom teachers provides access to video clips of evidence-based literacy instruction being implemented in classrooms throughout their state. Educators also have the opportunity to view live commentary from reading experts who help to explain the practice of teaching reading. They can provide information and visible teaching examples that are directly applicable to classroom activities. The objective of the on-line network is to provide users with a comprehensive application tool that utilizes research-based information and best practices on reading instruction. It provides a resource for literacy leadership teams to better understand what effective instruction looks like. In this way, they can more effectively replicate these practices within their school.

K–12 Reading Endorsement

A K–12 reading endorsement initiative is the final important piece of a statewide system of professional learning opportunities and can serve to build capacity for reading and literacy knowledge at each school. The statewide K–12 reading endorsement provides teachers, literacy coaches, and administrators with free on-line professional learning, including course offerings for language and cognition, research-based practices, assessment, and application of differentiated instruction. For literacy leadership teams that prefer a face-to-face experience in order to build capacity in each school district, the university-based area coordinators also provide facilitator in-service for the K–12 reading endorsement, including a clinical mentor in-service for supervision of a practicum.

Principal and Teacher Preparation

It is extremely important that graduate coursework adequately prepare principals in literacy leadership (both organizational and instructional supports) so that they can support schoolwide literacy initiatives. State departments of education must work with colleges of education to revise program requirements and principal certification exams to include the role of literacy leadership and, specifically, the advantages of a distributed cognition model like literacy leadership teams.

This same premise holds true for teacher preparation programs. The state must work closely with colleges of education to clearly articulate the importance of extensive training for elementary teachers to teach reading and coursework that provides all middle and high school teachers with the knowledge and skills to support literacy instruction in *all* content areas for *all* students. Only with this knowledge and these skills will teachers have the foundation to become literacy leaders within their schools.

University Faculty Fellows

Another support tool states can provide to colleges of education is the establishment of a collaborative consisting of literacy faculty from each of the state's teacher preparation programs that meet on a regularly scheduled basis. This group should be charged with collaborating with the university-based area coordinators to conduct literacy research in schools throughout the state. The research can then be used to inform the professional learning work of the area coordinators, as well as the teacher preparation work of the faculty at their respective institutions. This synergistic model of support helps colleges of education to stay closely connected to the needs of the K–12 system and the students and teachers within that system.

Access to Data

One final key element that states and school districts must help to pro-vide to school-level literacy leadership teams is assessment data that truly informs decision-making. Beyond the state-level outcome assessment data, states need to provide schools with progress monitoring data to assist school-level teams with determining whether instructional activities are being effective and what additional professional learning is necessary to make improvements in student outcomes. These assessments should include both group and individually administered measures of fluency, vocabulary, and comprehension. Plans should be in place for a comprehensive assessment system that will meet the needs of all students and educators in kindergarten through twelfth grade. Additionally, states and districts need to provide timely access to data through a statewide network to monitor student progress, a free data reporting tool for all schools to use to assist in instructional decision making.

Summary

It is extremely important that states begin to conduct research and highlight those schools and literacy leadership teams that have successfully changed the culture of their schools, moving toward a focus on literacy and collaboration, with a special emphasis on those schools that work with our most challenging populations of students. It is also extremely important to listen to and learn from these powerful exemplars, thus promoting state-level collaboration and modeling effective professional learning. As a part of this research, states should provide grants to exemplary literacy leadership teams to support their important work and then empower other leaders to implement those effective practices supported by the research.

As states begin to identify those schools that are doing exceptionally well (as compared to others with similar demographics), patterns of leadership should surface, particularly around the idea of distributed leadership through the literacy leadership team. States should form a group of principals who are able to articulate how they effectively built these teams to serve as a beacon and a stable resource of guidance and professional learning for faculty across the school. This is extremely important for many schools that have high levels of challenge, both in the student and teacher populations. Principals often describe past professional learning initiatives that failed because they had not built the capacity at the school to sustain efforts once the consultants left the building. Additionally, because the professional learning initiatives had not been driven by the teachers at the school level (as is the case with the literacy leadership teams), buy-in was extremely difficult to build as teachers gave up on practices before they had given them an opportunity to work. *The vested nature of the literacy leadership teams allows for a greater chance of successful implementation and sustainability.*

"Without someone with an informed vision of what good literacy instruction entails leading the charge, instructional change is likely to be beset with problems" (Biancarosa & Snow, 2004, p. 21). Teachers play a crucial role in ensuring the success of school-level literacy reforms. It is vital that states begin to change their perception that the focus should be on just one instructional leader in each school. Just as the principal must still be a co-driver of the instructional bus, or at least running in the forefront moving and removing potential roadblocks, states and districts must begin to see this as an important function as they work to support school literacy reform and the literacy leadership teams.

Both state and district leadership can support the work of successful literacy leadership teams by supporting the concept of professional learning and by a willingness to adjust practices and policies that may conflict with success at the school level. Only by ensuring that policymakers and district-level leadership are well grounded in issues related to literacy and the roles that must be played by the state, districts, principals, teachers, and higher education, can we truly impact literacy achievement for all students.

States and districts that wish to become effective facilitators of school-level professional learning and collaboration must themselves be strong models of this behavior. A state-level literacy initiative serves as an effective model through its coordination and collaboration with schools, districts, universities, and all the entities that support literacy throughout the state. As Schmoker (2006) states, "Organizations are either supported or constrained by those who exercise authority at the next highest level" (p. 151).

In conclusion, the literacy leadership team provides states and local districts a strong return on investment due to its strength in building capacity to incorporate research-based and evidence-based practices throughout the school. The ability to deliver consistent instruction and a shared sense of responsibility and efficacy across the school site cannot be underestimated as a means of serving the individual learning needs of students. The literacy leadership team provides the ongoing, job-embedded professional learning supported in the research literature. Although some may argue that teacher leadership initiatives pull our best teachers from their important classroom duties, Scherer (2007) prefers to view it as "expanding their reach" (p. 7). They continue to work within the classroom environment so that the classroom environment can sustain continued success, while sharing this success with their colleagues.

Final Note . . .

Learning and instructing imaginatively is imperative for literacy leadership teams to sustain and expand success. Although at times imagination is difficult to define succinctly, many educators will agree that it is the ability to create mental images or cognitive models, a primary function of literacy coaches and literacy leadership teams. Thus, without imagination, tackling adaptive challenges is an impossible act to accomplish. Imagination is central to any real educational enterprise (Egan & Nadnaer, 1988). Imagination is constructing mental models of possibilities (Frye, 1968).

Inspired and prompted primarily by the work of Maxine Greene and Elliot Eisner, mental models are generated by exposure and experience to a variety of texts (in-the-head and out-of-the-head) and cultures. The in-the-head texts, or invisible information, are the learner's language or cognitive lexical working system constructed by the learner over time. The out-of-the-head texts, or visible information, are all external input such as magazines, radio, television, books, and so on that learners use to evolve and transform. This input consequently feeds the imagination. It includes aural, olfactory, visual, kinesthetic, and tactile input. A variety of aural, olfactory, visual, kinesthetic, and tactile input has the potential to jump-start the imagination by taking learners to imaginary models of possibilities. Many of us have had the experience of hearing a sound or smelling a scent and the experience transported us into a dimension of our minds. Those experiences jump-started our imaginations and prompted us to create mental models that served us to imagine other models or situations.

As a member of a literacy leadership team, using your imagination is a critical point of consideration to process information efficiently and effectively in a society where information is updated, uploaded, and downloaded in nanoseconds, when our goal is tackling adaptive challenges. Therefore, in order for literacy leadership teams to process information efficiently, they must be able to predict and anticipate with sound criteria. Devoid of the capability to imagine, predicting and anticipating are virtually nonexistent (Greene, 1995). Consequently, any information processing attempted will not be processed efficiently, increasing the likelihood that information will be forgotten or misunderstood. Without imagination to power predicting and anticipating (the emotional hook that assists us in taking information from short-term memory to long-term memory), processing is stunted and prevents the development of a self-extending system (Clay, 2001), minimizing the likelihood of expanding success.

We firmly believe that only the individual is in control of his or her learning, and we recognize that knowledge is socially constructed (Vygotsky, 1978). Moreover, interexistentiality is impossible without imagination (Greene, 1995). Although we do understand that there is a strong connection between routines, rituals, facts, figures, and imagination (Egan, 1989), an over-the-top focus on routines, rituals, facts, and figures can be detrimental to learning, since learning in and of itself is essentially an imaginative endeavor (Egan, 1989).

Abundant research supports that programs do not make the difference, the teacher does. In addressing learning and instruction imaginatively, serious consideration needs to be given to the kinds of input that learners are being exposed to in any program of study. While addressing learning and instruction imaginatively, facts, figures, rituals, and routines are as critical as what is unsaid and need to be created by the learner. Facts, figures, rituals, and routines rely on our memory (or memories) and support exercising our memory. Imagination and memory cannot be thought of as paradoxical or dichotomous (Egan, 1989). Memories are necessary to imagine new possibilities, and imagination is necessary, in many cases, to remember (Eisner, 1998). What is unsaid and needs to be created by the learner relies on the learner's ability to imagine and infer. It is what is unsaid and needs to be created by the learner that will support the learner in extrapolating information by imagining alternatives (Eisner, 1998).

Time is usually a major concern in schools. Any school principal or classroom teacher will say that there is never enough time to "do" everything that needs to be done. First, in addressing the concern, we have to recognize that the concerns are being expressed and there seems to be a legitimate reality that needs to be dealt with, at least for the individuals who have expressed the concern. Once again, ironically, the solution to the concern is dependent on what we are trying to teach. It will take imagination to confront and consider alternatives in an already packed classroom and school schedule.

The second concern in tackling adaptive challenges imaginatively is *ownership*. When the people responsible for implementing a program of study—in this case, teachers—are not included in the design and development, it is more likely to meet resistance for implementation. The imaginative teacher will take it and run with it, but what about the veteran teacher who has been insulated from using her or his imagination for an extended period because of published sequenced materials? We are not being critical of published sequenced materials, but a constant diet of such programs does have an effect on an individual's pedagogy. In the past few years, we have seen many teachers ignore and sacrifice their experience and conventional wisdom to a program. Additionally, the issue of ownership presents itself when features and benefits are misunderstood. Seldom are the benefits of initiatives presented to classroom teachers in current professional learning practices. The focus is usually on the features of the initiatives with the benefits possibly addressed as a side effect. Here, education should take its lead from the business world and always promote the benefits to the consumer first.

The third concern for literacy leadership teams in addressing adaptive challenges imaginatively is *response.* Since the act of learning and instruction has such potential to be an esoteric practice, responding to administrators, teachers, students, and parents may be viewed as abstract a concept as black holes in space. The interactive act of responding in learning and instruction is crucial. Based on the work of Cambourne (1988), we prefer to use the term *response* instead of *feedback* because feedback may have mechanistic and didactic connotations that may contradict or stifle the act of learning and instruction. In acknowledging response, we need to accept that in the realm of learning and instruction, response is necessary to further the act of learning and instruction. After all, the act of learning and instruction is all about giving and taking. Yet, because learning and instruction are always open for interpretation, regardless of how well defined they can be, it may put those involved in the act on edge for fear of saying the wrong thing.

Although time, ownership, and response are not just inherent issues to learning and instruction, they are three major issues closely tied to the work of literacy leadership teams. Like any problem in virtually any field, the answer may appear simple on the surface. The reality of it is that learning and instruction is an abstract and complex concept open for interpretation where nuances are not easily measurable in a field that prides itself on quantitative and qualitative research. Thus, the issues are compounded with other curricular factors such as socioeconomic status, and mobility rates (administrators', teachers', and students') are complex. The optimist in us views these concerns and issues as hurdles to overcome instead of walls to tear down. All three major concerns—time, ownership, and response—certainly have and can generate imaginative solutions with the potential for long-term effects in your schools to sustain and expand success.

Based on the work of noted researchers in education, we started this book by defining learning and instruction while standing on the shoulders of giants in the field of education. Throughout the process, we had to keep reining in our imaginations to stay on the path we intended in order to generate an insightful and imaginative guide for you. Overall, the point that we are arguing for is that educators need to address adaptive challenges imaginatively if their desired goal is to school and educate students to be critical, effective, and efficient processors of information at a time when information availability is increasing exponentially.

Without the ability to construct these mental models of possibilities, not only will students be incapable of acquiring academic knowledge but they will also lack the motivation and interest to expand and extend their own body of knowledge. The same principle applies to literacy leadership teams. The goal should be to develop a self-monitoring, self-regulating, and self-extending system that will serve the team in the future.

We have also posited the argument that if we are to consider tackling adaptive challenges imaginatively, it has to come from a pedagogic-andragogic continuum of instruction. Literacy coaches and literacy leadership teams need to address learning and instruction that take all learners (adults and children) from subject-centered lessons to solution-seeking lessons that will promote and prompt minds to think beyond the conventional in all academic and nonacademic areas. Thinking outside the box is not sufficient anymore. We need to be able to construct our own metaphorical boxes to think outside of.

Although other issues and concerns could certainly have been addressed in this summary, we categorized universal organizational issues into time, ownership, and response. We extrapolated issues and challenges, based on available literature, personal experiences, literacy leadership team activities, and interactions with novice and experienced classroom teachers over many years. Administrators and teachers consistently have shared concerns about how much can they cram into a 6½-hour day for their students that will have lasting effects. The second category of concerns falls into ownership and the issue of a top-down management that may be appropriate in some schools but without modifications may be inappropriate in another school.

No one can deny that the imagination is what has created all the niceties that we take advantage of in our society. Our imaginations make us appreciate an Academy Award performance or a Van Gogh. Our imaginations bring tears of joy or sadness when reading Anita Diamant's *The Red Tent* or Dan Brown's *The Da Vinci Code*. As a literacy leadership team, use your imagination and tackle those adaptive challenges. The primary purpose of the literacy leadership team is to stimulate an awareness of the questionable. Its focus is two-fold: to create a predictive culture of learning and instruction, and to transfer the passion. To accomplish all that takes imagination. The jobs of teachers, literacy coaches, literacy leadership teams, and principals *are* complex, but the mission is simple: TRANSFER THE PASSION!

Appendix A
Literacy Leadership Team Self-Assessment Survey

The Literacy Leadership Team Self-Assessment Survey is designed for schools interested in utilizing a literacy leadership team supported by a literacy coach. This survey is but one instrument that supports schools in taking inventory of what is in place to promote forward shifts in learning and instruction. Assessment, particularly self-assessment, is a critical first step in determining where to start. After completing the survey, the total number of "very accurate" and "accurate" responses will provide you with a general idea of the present potential to sustain and expand success at your school. It is a starting point, not a determining point.

Schools are complex systems for learning and instruction, influenced by politics, economics, languages, and cultures. No single instrument of assessment can ever truly provide the necessary information to promote transformations in learning and instruction. This survey is meant to be cross-checked or triangulated with participant and nonparticipant observations to arrive at an accurate picture of existing strengths and needs.

Directions: Mark the statement that best describes your school. After completing the survey, total the number of "very accurate" and "accurate" responses.

1. The school Literacy Leadership Team consists of representatives from a variety of grade levels and/or content areas.

   ❏ very accurate   ❏ accurate   ❏ somewhat accurate   ❏ inaccurate   ❏ very inaccurate

2. There is a district Literacy Leadership Team to collaborate with the school Literacy Leadership Team.

   ❏ very accurate   ❏ accurate   ❏ somewhat accurate   ❏ inaccurate   ❏ very inaccurate

3. The Literacy Coach is the "lead learner" responsible for the professional learning of the school faculty and Literacy Leadership Team.

   ❏ very accurate   ❏ accurate   ❏ somewhat accurate   ❏ inaccurate   ❏ very inaccurate

4. The school Literacy Leadership Team investigates multiple sources of data (static and dynamic) to determine students' strengths and needs.

   ❏ very accurate   ❏ accurate   ❏ somewhat accurate   ❏ inaccurate   ❏ very inaccurate

5. The school Literacy Leadership Team investigates multiple sources of data (static and dynamic) to determine faculty and staff's strengths and needs.

   ❏ very accurate   ❏ accurate   ❏ somewhat accurate   ❏ inaccurate   ❏ very inaccurate

6. The school Literacy Leadership Team determines a specific adaptive challenge for the school or each grade level or content area based on data (static and dynamic).

   ❏ very accurate   ❏ accurate   ❏ somewhat accurate   ❏ inaccurate   ❏ very inaccurate

7. An action plan has been developed based on analyzed data (static and dynamic) by the Literacy Leadership Team.

    ❏ very accurate   ❏ accurate   ❏ somewhat accurate   ❏ inaccurate   ❏ very inaccurate

8. The school principal and the literacy coach attend all Literacy Leadership Team meetings.

    ❏ very accurate   ❏ accurate   ❏ somewhat accurate   ❏ inaccurate   ❏ very inaccurate

9. The school Literacy Leadership Team meets monthly for at least one hour.

    ❏ very accurate   ❏ accurate   ❏ somewhat accurate   ❏ inaccurate   ❏ very inaccurate

10. The school's action plan includes a five-stage implementation framework to ensure sustainability and expansion.

    ❏ very accurate   ❏ accurate   ❏ somewhat accurate   ❏ inaccurate   ❏ very inaccurate

11. The school has a designated block of time for reading/language arts.

    ❏ very accurate   ❏ accurate   ❏ somewhat accurate   ❏ inaccurate   ❏ very inaccurate

12. The school provides an intervention outside of the regular literacy block of time or language arts period for low-progress students.

    ❏ very accurate   ❏ accurate   ❏ somewhat accurate   ❏ inaccurate   ❏ very inaccurate

10–12	very accurate or accurate statements:	Strong potential for sustaining and expanding success
8–9	very accurate or accurate statements:	Above-average potential for sustaining and expanding success
6–7	very accurate or accurate statements:	Developing potential for expanding and sustaining success
4–5	very accurate or accurate statements:	Below-average potential for expanding and sustaining success
2–3	very accurate or accurate statements:	Weak potential for sustaining and expanding success

Note: The Literacy Leadership Team Self-Assessment Survey is meant to prompt and guide discussion. It was not designed or intended to serve as an evaluative instrument.

Appendix B
Five-Stage Plan for Sustaining and Expanding Success

Stage 1: Development of the Literacy Principal	Five full-day (30 hrs.) professional learning sessions that include classroom briefings, observations, and debriefings ■ Day 1: Literacy as a process and instructional practice ■ Day 2: Using assessment to guide instruction ■ Day 3: Coaching as a continuum of professional learning ■ Day 4: Transformational vs. interactive professional learning ■ Day 5: Organizing for instruction Recommended professional text: *(see Annotated Bibliography, Appendix D)*
Stage 2: Development of Literacy Leadership Team	5 full-day (30 hrs.) professional learning sessions ■ Day 1: Reading as a process and assessment ■ Day 2: Writing as a process and assessment ■ Day 3: Literacy as a process across content areas ■ Day 4: Teaching for reciprocity across content areas ■ Day 5: Creating a professional learning plan that includes a literacy coach Recommended professional text: *(see Annotated Bibliography, Appendix D)*
Stage 3: Job-Embedded Professional Learning of the Literacy Coach	■ 15 graduate-level credits/year-long, or 300 professional development hrs./year-long ■ Case study on high-, average-, and low-progress students ■ Videotape lessons with written reflections ■ *Scaffold study groups* at school level on literacy acquisition and development ■ Teach students on a daily basis ■ Participate in a summer literacy institute ■ Develop course for on-site professional learning in collaboration with the literacy leadership team based on vertical and horizontal assessment Recommended professional text: *(see Annotated Bibliography, Appendix D)*
Stage 4: Job-Embedded Professional Learning of Teachers	■ 40 hrs. on-site professional learning opportunity provided by literacy coach ■ Literacy coach continues to teach students on a daily basis ■ Literacy leadership team continues to reflect on data ■ 36 hrs. ongoing professional learning for literacy coach ■ Ongoing collaboration with literacy coach and literacy leadership team Recommended professional text: *(see Annotated Bibliography, Appendix D)*
Stage 5: Collaborative Action Research	■ 20 hrs. professional learning opportunity provided by literacy coach ■ Literacy coach continues to teach students on a daily basis ■ Literacy leadership team conducts schoolwide action research supported by literacy coach ■ 36 hrs. ongoing professional learning for literacy coach Recommended professional texts: *(see Annotated Bibliography, Appendix D)*

Appendix C
Action Plan for Intentional Literacy Instruction

Specific adaptive challenge identified:
Short-term and long-term assessments:
Grade levels impacted:
Resources needed:
Action steps/timetable:
Alternative action steps:
Reflections:

Appendix D
Annotated Bibliography

Literacy Leadership

The Literacy Principal: Leading, Supporting, and Assessing Reading and Writing Initiatives, second edition. Booth, D., & Rowsell, J. (2007). Pembroke Publishing.

This revised and expanded second edition challenges principals to become even more involved in becoming literacy leaders. It examines the role of school leaders at both the elementary and secondary levels. Commentaries from teachers, principals, and consultants who have been involved in developing strong schoolwide and districtwide literacy programs are included to demonstrate the progress many schools have made in the past few years. The increasingly important role of school literacy coaches along with literacy leadership teams is highlighted. Grounded in research and real-world experience, this new edition provides practical frameworks that principals can use in their quest to create schools where literacy learning is at the forefront of all instruction.

The K–12 Literacy Leadership Fieldbook. Taylor, R. T., & Gunter, G. A. (2005). Corwin Press.

This fieldbook sets forth a plan for improving literacy for students from kindergarten through high school. *The K–12 Literacy Leadership Fieldbook* demonstrates a process for creating a fail-safe approach to literacy that results in measurable improvement. Blending leadership with in-depth literacy knowledge, Taylor and Gunter show educators how to improve literacy through using software and technology integration to enhance curriculum and instruction; collaborating to set expectations for daily practice and a common language to drive instruction; using data to determine what works and what doesn't in your literacy program; and developing a fail-safe literacy point of view throughout your school

Literacy Learning Communities: A Guide for Creating Sustainable Change in Secondary Schools. Lent, R. C. (2007). Heinemann.

Schools nationwide are using professional learning communities to revitalize staff development.

Throughout *Literacy Learning Communities,* Lent provides suggestions for working with resistant faculty, overcoming a schoolwide culture of isolation (a particular problem in secondary schools), and strengthening the professional relationships in schools to improve the efficacy of LLCs. She presents Questions for Reflection at the end of each chapter to stimulate thinking and help schools move toward relevant and *sustained* professional learning. Built on a combination of research and real-world experience, *Literacy Learning Communities* can help build a culture of professional learning, peer support, and teacher engagement that will improve the performance of every learner—teacher and students alike.

Literacy Coaching

The Literacy Coach: Guiding in the Right Direction. Puig, E. A., & Froelich, K. S. (2007). Allyn and Bacon.

The book begins by situating literacy coaching within the larger perspective of professional learning. Defining literacy coaches as ethnographers, Puig and Froelich suggest that coaches rely on three forms of descriptive evidence: artifacts, nonparticipant observation, and participant observation experiences. They developed a "Continuum of Coaching" that outlines potential kinds of "coaching" that can be done. Three broad categories for the coaching of teachers are outlined: coaching for theoretical understanding, coaching for aesthetic understanding, and coaching for procedural understanding. Puig and Froelich then describe a five-year plan for developing and implementing a literacy coaching program at the elementary and middle/high school levels. The plans emphasize the use of study groups and the topics that they might cover somewhat more than doing individual coaching in teachers' classrooms. Careful reading and discussion of this book can help a school or district begin to develop a successful coaching program.

Literacy Coaching: The Essentials. Casey, K. (2006). Heinemann.

Casey has worked in school reform projects in both San Diego and New York City. In the foreword to the book, Alvarado captures well an important feature of this book: "A careful reader of this book will have made a professional colleague of the author." When planning, coaching, or debriefing, readers will continually ask, "What would Katherine say?" The opening of this book will really help new coaches get started. The book contains ideas that even the most experienced coach will find useful. The form that Casey suggests for note taking is excellent. Her chart of coaching cycles that use "to, with, and by" is worth much thought. Her ideas for intra-visitations and inter-visitations and "Push Pause" are useful for extending coaching from one-to-one sessions to groups of teachers.

The Literacy Coach's Handbook: A Guide to Research-Based Practice. Walpole, S., & McKenna, M. C. (2004). Guilford Press.

This comprehensive guide presents information to help literacy coaches meet the demands of designing and directing an elementary reading program. Step by step, the book provides the knowledge needed to ensure that teachers and students benefit from the concepts and methods emerging from scientifically based reading research. Reproducible figures and many detailed examples illustrate best practices for collecting and analyzing school-level data; selecting and organizing new curricula, texts, and resources; conducting ongoing professional learning to providing assistance to individual teachers; and engaging the whole school community in supporting positive change.

Literacy Instruction

Teaching for Comprehending and Fluency, K–8. Fountas, I. C., & Pinnell, G. S. (2006). Heinemann.

Teaching for Comprehending and Fluency, K–8 supports you with frameworks for high-quality instruction that describe appropriate expectations for comprehending, fluency, and vocabulary development. Fountas and Pinnell's teaching and assessment frames will give you a firm understanding of your students' reading levels: where they are, where they should be, and what they need to do to get there—for any reader, in any grade, at any moment. You'll also gain insight about the specific demands that fiction and nonfiction texts place on readers and about how effective readers think *within* a text, *beyond* a text, and *about* a text to gain rich understandings. Fountas and Pinnell's teaching tips, proven classroom ideas, and professional-learning opportunities will lead the way to help students develop effective systems of strategic actions over time.

Reading & Writing in the Middle Years, Booth, D. (2001). Stenhouse Publishers.

This comprehensive book is a no-nonsense exploration of successful approaches to teaching reading and writing to students in grades 4 to 8. The book begins with the basic information teachers need for understanding the reading and writing processes, and offers techniques for making literacy events meaningful to these growing students. Teachers will also find practical suggestions for expanding and monitoring comprehension, and designing instructional frameworks for supporting these developing readers and writers. Because students at this level are reading more and more in the content areas, the book includes suggestions for making all forms of nonfiction more meaningful for them. Rubrics, assessment checklists, and a targeted book list complement this accessible resource.

Creating Literacy-Rich Schools for Adolescents. Ivey, G., & Fisher, D. (2006). ASCD.

Ivey and Fisher state that all teachers have a role to play in students' development of literacy, which they define as reading, writing, speaking, listening, and viewing. Rather than focusing solely on reading instruction and the cliché that says "all teachers are teachers of reading," they urge teachers to incorporate rich literacy-based learning experiences into their classrooms, with the goal of helping students learn and think across the curriculum. Essential questions provide the focus for each chapter, and Quality Indicators for Secondary Literacy help readers gauge where they are on a continuum of providing a meaningful literacy experience for students. Rather than being overwhelmed by the challenge of improving literacy at the secondary level, readers will be inspired to move ahead with confidence that the task is essential, worthwhile, and achievable.

Glossary

Acronym method: Using the "letters" of one word, the group determines the features that are important so that the team can achieve success through discussion and collaboration.

Action steps: The who, what, and when in the implementation of an action plan.

Adaptive challenge: Improvement issues that serve as a learning experience with the potential for transformation and forward shifts.

Advanced readers: Students who have achieved independence and have developed self-improving systems.

Andragogy: The art and science of instruction and learning with adults.

Assessment for learning: Documented data used in the classroom that show how students are learning. These are generally dynamic types of measurements showing how students are processing information.

Assessment of learning: Documented data that show what students have learned. These are generally static outcome measurements.

Brookfield & Preskill's method: Group members consider the positive and negative things that can affect how a group works. They come up with three things that they believe will help create positive change.

Collaborative writing: An instructional practice where the teacher and the students engage in writing a text together.

Comprehensive literacy plan: The plan of action that the leadership develops that covers a wide variety of topics and extends over a long period of time.

Conditions for learning: Circumstances that can be created to promote learning.

Co-triangulation: Cross-checking overlapping data.

Developing readers: Learners that are acquiring basic book handling skills and are just learning that illustrations and books tell a story.

Discussion groups (also called discussion circles, literature circles, and book-talk groups): These groups are generally centered on the reading of a single text either by author, title, or theme so that members can discuss concepts that promote a deeper understanding of the text.

Dynamic assessment: Documented survey, inventory, or record of how students are processing information over time.

Early readers: Learners who are developing strategic activities for reading and self-correcting.

Feedback: Monitoring, searching, and self-correcting.

Feedforward: Predicting and anticipating.

Forward shifts: Positive change; transformational movement that promotes growth.

Graphophonic working systems: In-the-head knowledge of letters and sounds.

Guided reading: An instructional practice incorporating small-group instruction utilizing text within students' zone of proximal development or instructional level.

Guided writing: An instructional practice incorporating small-group instruction with students having similar strengths and needs in the craft of writing.

Horizontal assessment: Documented survey, inventory, or record of how students are processing information over time used to guide instruction for strategic activity.

Independent reading: An instructional practice where students engage with texts of their own choice and for their own purposes with teacher support.

Independent writing: An instructional practice where students work on writing of their own choosing and for their own purposes with teacher support.

Information-intensive environment: A learning setting rich in on-line and off-line resources for students to learn.

Instructional practices: Teacher-initiated moves to support learning.

Intentional instruction: Thoughtful, systematic, and explicit instruction.

Interactive editing: An instructional practice where students are actively engaged with the teacher and peers in editing.

Interactive read-aloud: An instructional practice where students are actively engaged with the teacher and peers in brief conversations while the teacher reads aloud.

Interactive spelling: An instructional practice where students are actively engaged with the teacher and peers in learning how words work.

Interactive vocabulary study: An instructional practice where students are actively engaged with the teacher and peers in learning new words.

Interactive writing: An instructional practice where the teacher and the students "share the pen" to construct text that was collaboratively composed.

Language experience approach: An instructional approach where the teacher and the students compose and construct text based on lived experiences.

Lexical working system: In-the-head knowledge of receptive and productive vocabulary.

Literacy resource station: In project-centered classrooms, a specified area in intermediate, middle, and high school grades that provides students resources to engage in research.

Literacy workstation: A specified area for specific activities in primary classrooms (K–2) stocked with age-appropriate resources for students to use independently to promote self-regulation, self-direction, and practice.

Modeled reading: An instructional practice where a more knowledgeable other provides an opportunity for observation of what readers do when they engage with text.

Modeled writing: An instructional practice where a more knowledgeable other provides an opportunity for observation of what writers do as they compose and construct messages.

Pedagogy: The art and science of instruction and learning with children.

Pragmatic working systems: In-the-head knowledge of an author's intent.

Prior knowledge: Known information that can be used to enhance new information.

Reciprocity of literate activities: The act in which reading/writing practices support writing/reading practices.

Schematic working systems: In-the-head memories used to enhance new learning.

Self-extending readers: Learners who have systems in place for learning more about processing information as they read so that they build skills by encountering different genres with a variety of new vocabulary.

Self-improving system: A system that learners have in place when they are self-directed, self-regulated, and self-motivated.

Semantic feature analysis: A graphic organizer used for organizing information centered on one theme. It is a grid showing the connections between words in one category.

Shared reading: A highly supportive instructional practice with voice support while students are invited to read.

Small-group method: A method that asks group members to put their ideas about how groups work effectively on index cards and then reach consensus about which ones they think are the most important so that the group can be successful.

Static assessment: Documented survey, inventory, or record of what students have learned over time.

Strategic activities: A call to action initiated by the learner.

Syntactic working system: In-the-head knowledge of how language is organized grammatically.

Transferability: The ability to move one set of constructs so that it can meet the needs of another set so that we can use a common language when we work with others.

Transitional readers: Learners who have gained enough control of reading so that self-correction is automatic.

Vertical assessment: Documented survey, inventory, or record of what students have learned over time used to compare student progress aligned to grade-level expectations.

Word walls: An instructional practice used generally in primary grades (K–2) to support students in acquiring early reference skills.

References

Allen, J. (2006). *Becoming a literacy leader: Supporting learning and change*. Portland, ME: Stenhouse.

Allington, R., & Walmsley, S. (Eds.). (2007). *No quick fix, The RTI edition: Rethinking literacy programs in America's elementary schools*. New York: Teachers College Press.

Alvermann, D. (1996). Peer-led discussions: Whose interests are served? *Journal of Adolescent & Adult Literacy*, 39(4), 282–289.

Alvermann, D. E., Phelps, S. F., & Ridgeway, V. G. (2007). *Content area reading and literacy: Succeeding in today's diverse classrooms* (5th ed.). Boston: Pearson/Allyn and Bacon.

Anderson, R. C. (1985). The role of reader's schema in comprehension, learning and memory. In H. Singer & R. B. Ruddell (Eds.), *Theoretical models and processes of reading* (3rd ed.). Newark, DE: International Reading Association.

Ashton-Warner, S. (1965). *Teacher*. New York: Simon & Schuster.

Bandura, A. (1998). *Self-efficacy: The exercise of control*. New York: Freeman and Company.

Baldwin, R. S., Ford, J. C., & Readance, J. E. (1981). Teaching word connotation: An alternative strategy. *Reading World, 21*, 103–108.

Banta, T. W., et al. (1996). *Assessment in practice: Putting principles to work on college campuses*. San Francisco: Jossey-Bass.

Bennett, C. K. (1994, Winter). Promoting teacher reflection through action research: What do teachers think? *Journal of Staff Development 15*(1), 34–38.

Biancarosa, G., & Snow, C. E. (2004). *Reading next—A vision for action and research in middle and high school literacy: A report to Carnegie Corporation of New York*. Washington, DC: Alliance for Excellent Education

Birchak, B., Connor, C., Crawford, K., Kahn, L., Kayer, S., Turner, S., & Short, K. (1998). *Teacher study groups: Building community through dialog and reflection*. Urbana, IL: National Council of Teachers of English.

Booth, D., & Rowsell, J. (2002). *The literacy principal: Leading, supporting and assessing reading and writing initiatives*. Ontario, Canada: Pembroke Publishing.

Booth, D. & Rowsell, J. (2007). *The literacy principal: Leading, supporting and assessing reading and writing initiatives* (2nd ed.). Ontario, Canada: Pembroke Publishing.

Brookfield, S., & Preskill, S. (1999). *Discussion as a way of teaching: Tools and techniques for democratic classrooms*. San Francisco: Jossey-Bass.

Bruner, J. (1990). *Acts of meaning*. Cambridge, MA: Harvard University Press.

Burns, A. (1999). *Collaborative action research for English language teachers*. Cambridge, UK: Cambridge University Press.

Caine, R. N., & Caine, G. (1994). *Making connections: Teaching and the human brain*. New York: Addison-Wesley.

Cambourne, B. (2007). Biomimicry and educational innovation. *BioInspired!* Volume 5, No. 1. Retrieved from Weblog.

Cambourne, B. (1988). *The whole story: Natural learning and the acquisition of literacy in the classroom*. Auckland, New Zealand: Ashton-Scholastic.

Casey, K. (2006). *Literacy coaching: The essentials*. Portsmouth, NH: Heinemann.

Cazden, C. (1988). *Classroom discourse: The language of learning and instruction*. Portsmouth, MA: Heinemann.

Chall, J. S. (1983). *Stages of reading development*. New York: McGraw-Hill.

Clay, M. M. (1998). *By different paths to common outcomes*. York, ME: Stenhouse Publishers.

Clay, M. M. (2001). *Change over time in children's literacy development*. Portsmouth, NH: Heinemann.

Costa, A., & Garmston, R. (2002). *Cognitive coaching: A foundation for Renaissance schools*. Norwood, MA: Christopher-Gordon.

Craig, P. S. (2006). A descriptive analysis of the relationship between specific teacher characteristics and teacher efficacy in Florida's low-performing public high schools. Unpublished dissertation. University of South Florida.

Cross, K. P. (1981). *Adults as learners: Increasing participation and facilitating learning*. San Francisco: Jossey-Bass.

Cunningham, P. M., & Allington, R. L. (1998). *Classrooms that work: They can all read and write.* Boston: Allyn and Bacon.

Darling-Hammond, L. (1997). *The right to learn: A blueprint for creating schools that work.* San Francisco: Jossey Bass.

Deming, W. E. (2000). Condensation of the fourteen points for management. *Educational Leadership.* San Francisco: Jossey-Bass.

Deschler, D., Schumaker, J., & Woodruff, S. (2004). Improving literacy skills of at-risk adolescents. In D. S. Strickland & D. E. Alvermann (Eds.), *Bridging the literacy achievement gap grades 4–12* (pp. 86–106). New York: Teachers College Press.

Dixson-Krauss, L. (1996). *Vygotsky in the classroom: Mediated literacy instruction and assessment.* White Plains, NY: Longman.

Egan, K., & Nadnaer, D. (Eds.). (1988). *Imagination and education.* New York: Teachers College Press.

Egan, K. (1989, February). Memory, imagination and learning: Connected by the story. *Phi Delta Kappan,* 70(6), 455–459.

Egan, K. (2001, April). Start with what the student knows or with what the student can imagine? A paper presented at the annual AERA conference.

Eisner, E. (1998). *The kinds of schools we need.* Portsmouth, MA: Heinemann.

Fountas, I. C., & Pinnell, G. S. (2001). *Guiding readers and writers 3–6: Taeching comprehension, genre, and content literacy.* Portsmouth, NH: Heinemann.

Fountas, I. C. & Pinnell, G. S. (2006). *Teaching for comprehending and fluency: Thinking, talking and writing about reading (K–8).* Portsmouth, NH: Heinemann.

Frank, C. (1999). *Ethnographic eyes: A teacher's guide to classroom observations.* Portsmouth, NH: Heinemann.

Frayer, D., Frederick, W., & Klausmeier, H. (1969). A schema for testing the level of cognitive mastery (Working Paper No. 10). Madison, WI: Wisconsin Research and Development Center.

Frye, N. (1968). *The educated imagination.* Bloomington: Indiana University Press.

Fullan, M. (1994). Coordinating top-down and bottom-up strategies for educational reform. Retrieved October 7, 2007, from www.ed.gov/pubs/EdReformStudies/SysReforms/fullan1.html.

Fullan, M. (2000). *Change forces: The sequel.* Philadelphia: Falmer Press.

Fullan, M. (2005). *Leadership and sustainability: Systems thinkers in action.* Thousand Oaks, CA: Corwin Press.

Fullan, M., Hill, P., & Crevola, C. (2006). *Breakthrough.* Thousand Oaks, CA: Corwin Press.

Gaffney, J. S. & Askew, B. J. (1999). *Stirring the waters: The influence of Marie Clay.* Portsmouth, NH: Heinemann.

Gardner, J. W. (2000). The nature of leadership. *Educational Leadership.* San Francisco: Jossey-Bass.

Gillion, G. T. (2004). *Phonological awareness: From research to practice.* New York: Guilford Press.

Glanz, J. (2003). *Action research: An educational leader's guide to school improvement.* Norwood, MA: Christopher-Gordon.

Glasser, W. (2000). We need noncoercive lead-management from the state superintendent to the teacher. *Educational Leadership.* San Francisco: Jossey-Bass.

Gonzalez, N., Moll, L., & Amanti, C. (2005). *Funds of knowledge: Theorizing practices in households, communities, and classrooms.* Mahwah: NJ: Lawrence Erlbaum.

Greene, M. (1995). *Releasing the imagination.* San Francisco: Jossey-Bass.

Gunning, T. (2004). *Creating literacy for all children.* Boston: Allyn and Bacon.

Heifetz, R., & Linsky, M. (2002). *Leadership on the line: Staying alive through the dangers of leading.* Boston: Harvard Business School Press.

Hill, P. W., & Crevola, C. A. (1998). The role of standards in educational reform for the 21st century. In D. D. Marsh (Ed.), *ASCD Yearbook 1999: Preparing our schools for the 21st century* (pp. 117–142). Alexandria, VA: Association for Supervision and Curriculum Development.

Holdaway, D. (1979). *The foundations of literacy.* Gosford, New South Wales: Ashton Scholastic.

Hord, S. M. (1997). *Professional learning communities: Communities of continuous inquiry and development.* Austin, TX: Southwest Educational Development Laboratory.

Hubbard, R. S., & Powers, B. M. (1999). *Living the questions: A guide for teacher-researchers.* York, ME: Stenhouse.

Jarvis, P. (1987). *Adult learning in the social context.* London: Croom Helm.

Jensen, E. (1998). *Teaching with the brain in mind*. Alexandria, VA: Association of Supervision and Curriculum Development.

Johnson, D. W., & Johnson, R. T. (1999). *Learning together and alone*. Boston: Allyn and Bacon

Johnson, D. D., & Pearson, P. D. (1984). *Teaching reading vocabulary* (2nd ed.). New York: Holt, Rinehart and Winston.

Johnston, P. H. (1997). *Knowing literacy: Constructive literacy assessment*. York, ME: Stenhouse.

Johnston, P. H. (2004). *Choice words: How our language affects children's learning*. York, ME: Stenhouse.

Joyce, B., & Showers, B. (2003). *Student learning through staff development* (3rd ed.). Alexandria, VA: Association for Supervision and Curriculum Development.

Keene, E., & Zimmerman, S. (1997). *Mosaic of thought*. Portsmouth, NM: Heineman.

Kellough, R. D., & Kellough, N. G. (1999). *Secondary school seaching: A guide to methods and resources: Planning for competence*. Upper Saddle River, NJ: Prentice-Hall.

Kemmis, S., & McTaggart, R. (1988). *The action research planner* (3rd ed.). Geelong, Victoria, Australia: Deakin University Press.

Knight, J. (2007). *Instructional coaching: A partnership approach to improving instruction*. Thousand Oaks, CA: Corwin Press.

Knight, S. L., & Stallings, J. A. (1995). The implementation of the accelerated school model in an urban elementary school. In R. L. Allington & S. A. Walmsley (Eds.), *No quick fix: Rethinking literacy programs in America's elementary schools* (pp. 236–251). New York: Teachers College Press.

Knowles, M. S. (1978). *The adult learner: A neglected species*. Houston, TX: Gulf.

Knowles, M., Holton, E. E., & Swanson, R. A. (2005). *The adult learner: The definitive classic in adult education and human resource development*. Boston: Elsevier, Butterworth, Heinemann.

Knox, A. B. (1980). Proficiency Theory of Adult Learning. *Contemporary Educational Psychology, 5*, 378–404.

Lambert, L. (2003). *Leadership capacity for lasting school improvement*. Alexandria, VA: Association for Supervision and Curriculum Development.

Langer, J. A. (2000). *Effective literacy instruction: Building successful reading and writing programs*. Urbana, IL: National Council of Teachers of English.

Lave, J. (1988). *Cognition in practice*. New York: Cambridge Press.

Lave, J. & Wenger, E. (1991). *Situated learning*. New York: Cambridge Press.

Lent, R. C. (2007). *Literacy learning communities: A guide for creating sustainable change in secondary schools*. Portsmouth, NH: Heinemann.

Lieberman, A., Saxl, E. R., & Miles, M. B. (2000). Building a professional culture in school. *Educational Leadership*. San Francisco: Jossey-Bass.

Lindeman, E. (1961). *The meaning of adult education*. New York: Harvest House.

Lyons, C. A. & Pinnell, G. S. (2001). *Systems for change in literacy education: A guide to professional learning*. Portsmouth, NH: Heinemann.

Maden, M. (2001). Further lessons in success. In M. Maden (Ed.), *Success against the odds—Five years on* (pp. 307–339). London: Routledge.

Maden, M., & Hillman, J. (1996). *Success against the odds*. London: Routledge.

Maiese, M. (2004). Ground rules. In G. Burgess & H. Burgess (Eds.), *Beyond intractability*. Conflict Research Consortium, University of Colorado, Boulder. Retrieved September 10, 2007, from www .beyondintractibility.org/essay.

McCarrier, A., Fountas, I. C., & Pinnell, G. S. (1999). *Interactive writing: How language & literacy come together, K–2*. Portsmouth, NH: Heinemann.

McClusky, H. Y. (1970). An Approach to a differential psychology of the adult potential. In S. M. Grabowski (Ed.), *Adult learning and instruction*. Syracuse, NY: ERIC Clearinghouse on Adult Education.

McClusky, H. Y. (1963). The course of the adult life span. In W. C. Hallenbeck (Ed.), *Psychology of adults*. Washington, DC: Adult Education Association.

Merriam, S. B., & Caffarella, R. S. (1999). *Learning in adulthood: A comprehensive guide*. San Francisco: Jossey-Bass.

Mills, G. E. (2003). Action research: A guide for the teacher researcher. Upper Saddle River, NJ: Merrill/Prentice Hall.

Mooney, M. E. (1990). *To, with, and by*. Katonah, NY: Richard C. Owens Publishers.

National Reading Panel. (2000). *Teaching children to read: An evidence-based assessment of the scientific research literature on reading and its implications for reading instruction.* Washington, DC: National Institute for Literacy and The Partnership for Reading.

Pearson, P. D. & Gallagher, M. C. (1983). The instruction of reading comprehension. *Contemporary Educational Psychology, 8,* 317–344.

Pinnell, G. S. & Fountas, I. C. (1998). *Word matters: Teaching phonics and spelling in the reading/writing classroom.* Portsmouth, NH: Heinemann.

Pressley, M. (2002). *Reading instruction that works: The case for balanced teaching.* New York: Guilford Press.

Puig, E. A., & Froelich, K. S. (2007). *The literacy coach: Guiding in the right direction.* Boston: Pearson/Allyn and Bacon.

Rosenblatt, L. (1994). *The reader, the text, and the poem: The transactional theory of the literary work.* Carbondale: Southern Illinois University Press.

Rosenthal, R., & Jacobson, L. (1968). *Pygmalian in the classroom.* New York: Holt, Rinehart and Winston.

Ross, J. A. (1992). Teacher efficacy and the effects of coaching on student achievement. *Canadian Journal of Education, 17*(1), 51–65.

Rushton, S. P., Eitelgeorge, J., & Zickafoose, R. (2003). Connecting Brian Cambourne's conditions of learning theory to brain/mind principles: Implications for early childhood educators. *Early Childhood Education Journal, 31*(1), 11–21.

Scherer, M. (2007). Playing to strengths. *Educational Leadership, 65*(1), 7.

Schmoker, M. (2006). *Results now: How we can achieve unprecedented improvements in learning and instruction.* Alexandria, VA: Association for Supervision and Curriculum Development.

Schwartz, R. (1988). Learning to learn vocabulary in content area textbooks. *Journal of Reading, 32,* 108–117.

Senge, P. M. (1990). *The fifth discipline: The art & practice of the learning organization.* New York: Doubleday.

Senge, P. M. (2000). *"Give me a lever long enough . . . and single-handed I can move the world." Educational Leadership.* San Francisco: Jossey-Bass.

Sergiovanni, T. J. (2000). Leadership as Stewardship: "Who's Serving Who?" *Educational Leadership.* San Francisco: Jossey-Bass.

Shuler, D. (2002). Uncovering and understanding our common language. *Community Technology Review.* Retrieved from www.trout.cpsr.org.

Smith, F. (1981). Demonstrations, engagement, and sensitivity: A revised approach to language learning. *Language Arts, 58*(6), 634–642.

Spradley, J. P. (1980). *Participant observation.* Fort Worth, TX: Harcourt Brace Javonovich.

Stein, D. (1998). Situated learning in adult education. *ERIC Digest.* Retrieved from www.ericdigests.org.

Stigler, J., & Hiebert, J. (1999). *The teaching gap.* New York: The Free Press.

Stringer, E. (1996). *Action research: A handbook for practitioners.* Thousand Oaks, CA: Sage.

Taylor, R. T., & Gunter, G. A. (2006). *The K–12 literacy leadership fieldbook.* Thousand Oaks, CA: Corwin Press.

Teacher Today. (2003, March). Learning in groups. Volume 18, number 7.

Tharp, R. G., & Gallimore, R. (1988). *Rousing minds to life: Teaching, learning, and schooling in social context.* Cambridge, England: Cambridge University Press.

"Tips for Working Successfully in a Group." (2001). Retrieved September 10. 2007, from www.alice.org.

Toll, C. A. (2004). *The literacy coach's survival guide: Essential questions and practical answers.* Newark, DE: International Reading Association.

Tomlinson, C. (2001). *How to differentiate instruction in mixed-ability classrooms* (2nd ed.). Alexandria, VA: Association for Supervision and Curriculum Development.

Tschannen-Moran, M. (2004). *Trust matters: Leadership for successful schools.* San Francisco: Jossey-Bass.

Veenman, S. & Denessen, E. (2001). The coaching of teachers: Results of five training studies. *Educational Research and Evaluation, 7*(4), 385–417.

Vygotsky, L. S. (1978). *Mind in society: The development of higher psychological processes.* Cambridge, MA: Harvard University Press.

Walpole, S., & McKenna, M. C. (2004). *The literacy coaches handbook: A guide to research-based practice.* New York: Guilford.

Wolfe, P. (2001). *Brain matters: Translating research into classroom practice.* Alexandria, VA: Association for Supervision and Curriculum Development.

Young, M. F. (1993). Instructional design for situated learning. *Educational Technology Research and Development, 41*(1), 43–58.

Index

M

Margin, theory of (related to adult learning) (McClusky), 11
Meaning, constructing, and expanding, 53–54
Media specialist on literacy leadership team, 88
Metacognitive working systems, 40–45
Modeled writing, 94

O

Observation as a condition for learning, 18–19
Observation classroom, co-teaching, 134–136
Observation lesson, providing, 133–134
Ongoing learning, 127–129
On-line literacy learning network, 160
Overteaching too many concepts, 107

P

Pedagogy vs. andragogy, 8–10
Positive interdependence, definition of, 115
Predictions and estimations as condition for learning, 20–21
Principals as members of literacy leadership team, 88, 127, 145, 146, 147
  preparation of, 161
Prior experiences, 41
Professional growth among literacy leadership team members, 68
Professional learning:
  "menu," 131
  ongoing and job-embedded, 127–129
  resources, 160
  scheduling activities, 128–129
Professional literature about literacy leadership teams, 88–89
Proficiency theory (related to adult learning) (Knox), 11–12
Prompting, 92
Purpose-driven learning, 9

R

Read-aloud as instructional practice, 90
Reading:
  activities to sustain, 45
  developmental stages of, 45–49
  focus-lesson for, 105
  as a process, 40–45

and writing, reciprocal nature of, 51
Receptive learning, 42–43
Reciprocity of literate activities, 51
Refining adaptive challenges (see Adaptive challenges)
Resources, selecting, 118–119, 120
Response:
  as a condition for learning, 21–22, 26
  vs. feedback, 166
Responsibility as a condition for learning, 19–20, 26
Risk taking, 24

S

Scaffolding instruction, 54
Schematic working system, 41
Schoolwide plan, developing, 143–154
Secondary (grades 6–12) literacy leadership teams, 69
Self-assessment survey for literacy leadership team, 60–61
Self-esteem in learners, 23
Self-extending readers, stage of development, 47
Semantic Feature Analysis, 33, 34
Semantic working system, 41
Sequencing story events, 93
Shared decision making, 115
Shared reading as instructional practice, 91–92
Situational learning, 12–13
Solution seeking, 20, 39, 53–54
Sounds and symbols, 40–41
Standardized tests, 79
State and district support, 155–163
  access to data, 161–162
  K–12 leadership conference, 158–159
  K–12 literacy coach academies, 159
  K–12 literacy plan, 157–158
  K–12 reading endorsement, 160–161
  principal and teacher preparation, 161
  professional learning resources, 160
  summer literacy leadership team institutes, 159
  university-based support, 158, 161
Static assessment, 54–55
  definition of, 86
Storyboard exercise, 93
Study group:
  developing, 113–119, 120

facilitating, 138–139
Summer literacy leadership team institutes, 159
Syntactic working system, 43

T

Teacher preparation programs for supporting literacy leadership teams, 161
Teaching for strategic activity, 52–55
Time, lack of, 165
Topic for study, reaching consensus on, 117–118
Transferability of definitions, 31
Transitional readers, stage of development, 47
Triadic model for literacy leadership teams, 2
Triangulation, definition of, 75

U

Understanding literacy, 67–68
Use/employment as a condition for learning, 24–25, 26

V

Vertical assessment of learning, 77
Vertical and horizontal assessment of learning and instruction, 101, 118, 119
Vocabulary:
  focus-lesson for, 107
  study, 33–34, 97

W

Words, knowledge of, 42–43
Words and concepts, relationships among, 31
Workshop facilitation by literacy coach, 130–132
Writer's workshop approach, 96
Writing:
  collaborative, 95
  focus-lesson for, 106
  as a process, 49–50
  revising, 49–50
  small-group instruction, 96

Y

Year-long course for classroom teachers, 149, 152
Year-long in-service for literacy coaches, 149, 150–151
Young learners vs. adult learners, 8, 10

Z

Zone of proximal development, 18, 52